Essential Ingredients

Recipes

for

Teaching

Writing

Sandra Worsham

ASCD Association for Supervision and Curriculum Development Alexandria, Virginia USA

Association for Supervision and Curriculum Development
1703 N. Beauregard St. • Alexandria, VA 22311-1714 USA
Telephone: 1-800-933-2723 or 703-578-9600 • Fax: 703-575-5400
Web site: http://www.ascd.org • E-mail: member@ascd.org

Printed in the United States of America.

ASCD Product No. 101241
ASCD member price: $19.95   nonmember price: $23.95

s12/2001

Library of Congress Cataloging-in-Publication Data
Worsham, Sandra, 1947–
Essential ingredients : recipes for teaching writing / Sandra Worsham.
    p. cm.
Includes bibliographical references and index.
"ASCD product no. 101241"—T.p. verso.
   ISBN 0-87120-594-7 (alk. paper)
   1. English language—Composition and exercises—Study and teaching—United States.   2. Creative writing—Study and teaching—United States.
I. Title.
   LB1576 .W6855 2001
   808'.042'071—dc21   2001005144

07 06 05 04 03 02 01   10 9 8 7 6 5 4 3 2 1

Edna Earle Fordham Worsham

My mother, Edna Worsham, was a wise woman who was full of wit and pithy observation. In 1995, my sister Linda and I lost her, at age 84, to ovarian cancer. During the time that Mama was ill, when speaking of her approaching death, she said, "It is just as important to prepare for death as to prepare for life," and "Life is just a book, and this is the grande finale."

Throughout this book, in the way that I recommend you share with your students, I share with you memories of my mother, my childhood, and my hometown of Milledgeville, Georgia.

As part of my memories, I share Mama's recipes and the stories that go along with them. This book is dedicated to the creator of the recipes and the one who shared her memories with me.

Essential Ingredients

Recipes for Teaching Writing

Preface

AMANDA, A COLLEGE SENIOR PREPARING TO BE AN ELEMENTARY SCHOOL TEACHER, writes about her experiences with writing:

> It began when I was in second grade, the year I was really intro-
> duced to poetry. I loved it. I started writing and couldn't stop. All
> my best friends would say, "Write a poem for me," and so I would.
> But though it seemed that everyone in my life loved my writings,
> my teachers didn't often encourage me.
>
> In my junior year in high school, a teacher shot all my confidence
> down by saying, "You have so much to learn about writing. Your
> grammar is bad, and you have a lot of run-on sentences." My heart
> was broken, and I began to feel that my loved ones had only
> praised my writing because they love me, not because I was good.

Kevin, a 3rd grader, says of writing, "I love writing at home, but I
hate it at school. At school, writing is boring. We just do the same
thing over and over again."

As a young teacher in the early 1970s, I liked to write. I got up
early in the morning to work on my stories; sometimes I took my
blue writing notebook to work, hoping that sometime during the
day I would have a minute to write a sentence or two. When calling
out words for spelling tests or reading a poem aloud to my class, I

*This is not my recipe.
This is a memory,
retrievable only as mem-
ories are, by evocation
and gesture and occa-
sional concreteness that
is not factual. And I
resist making it a recipe.
This is about art and
love, not about tech-
nique. Some things need
to be learned standing
beside someone.*

— Elizabeth Kamarck Minnich,
*"But Really, There Are No
Recipes,"* Through the Kitchen
Window, *p. 135*

often stopped and gazed out the window—flies buzzing, dog-woods full of cowbirds eating berries—and then to my blue note-book. I ached to add to it, somehow understanding my writing better during the day as my mind turned to other things. Yet, my dear writing notebook was strangely misplaced in that schoolroom. My writing was a sweet secret I carried with me.

On the other hand, I was a teacher of writing. In high school we taught an essay-writing formula to prepare students for college Eng-lish. Students learned the formula well but still had trouble with grammar. So I used the traditional correcting symbols and the hunt-and-shoot method of grading. If I could make all my students' essays exactly alike, I thought at the time, then I would have succeeded.

The problem was that these student essays, all clones of one another, were boring, just plain boring. Even when the mechanics and usage were impeccable, formula essays were just not interest-ing or entertaining to read. Looking back, I'm sure now that the essays were equally tedious for my students to write. In her intro-duction to *Writing Down the Bones,* Natalie Goldberg (1991a) writes of school writing: "I was a goody-two-shoes all through school. I wanted my teachers to like me. I learned commas, colons, semicolons. I wrote compositions with clear sentences that were dull and boring. Nowhere was there an original thought or genuine feeling" (p. 1).

After teaching for 10 years, I went back to school to work on my graduate degree and learned that the writing I did at home and the writing I taught at school did not have to be separate and apart. A quote from Dan Kirby and Tom Liner's *Inside Out* (1981) clarified this distinction for me.

> Academic writing too often is Engfish, Ken Macrorie's word for the lifeless, inhibited prose too often expected in English classes and read only by English teachers. It's pedantic and phony—and it's bad. It's so bad that we have to use external motivation to get the kids to do it.

"The grade school student is told by his teacher that he must learn Engfish because the high school teacher will expect mastery of it. The high school student is told by his teacher that he must learn it because the college professor will expect mastery of it. The college undergraduate is told by his professor that he must learn it so he can go to graduate school and write his PhD thesis in it. Almost no one reads PhD theses." (Ken Macrorie. *Uptaught*. Hayden, 1970.)

One reason Engfish is rampant is that writing in our schools has been essentially a neurotic exercise. We give the kids a writing assignment so we can tell them what's wrong with their writing. (p. 40)

Brenda Ueland (1987), in one of my all-time favorite books on writing—*If You Want to Write: A Book About Art, Independence, and Spirit*—says this another way:

We start out in our lives as little children, full of light and the clearest vision. . . . Then we go to school and then comes on the great Army of school teachers with their critical pencils . . . and finally that Great Murderer of the Imagination—a world of unceasing, unkind, dinky, prissy Criticalness. . . . But really it was teaching us grammar and spelling. They did not see that it was your true thought that is interesting, enchanting, important. (p. X–XI)

The most significant discovery I made during graduate school was that I could take out my blue notebook and read to my students straight from it and talk about this journey we are on together, that of learning to write well. I discovered that I could write with my students as equals and that they wrote more if I wrote with them. I also attended summer writers' conferences—Bread Loaf, Bennington, and Sewanee. I observed published writers helping one another with their writing. I decided that the kind of writing that successful writers do is the kind of writing we should be teaching in school.

Cooking is about more than food (and so is eating!).

—Judith Moore,
Never Eat Your Heart Out,
p. 236

What, then, characterizes the writing of published authors? What are the differences between the writing students do for fun and the writing they are taught in schools? If we teachers are to use the methods employed by successful writers, how will our teaching of writing change?

Bringing Real Writing to School

In this book, I identify four qualities that I believe writers use that we can pass on to our students: (1) appealing to the senses—especially taste, smell, and touch; (2) making use of our own locale and sense of place; (3) using our own memories and stories; and (4) expanding and changing the directions we follow to make our writing better.

Appealing to the Senses

When professional writers write, they appeal to the senses. Famous writers know that vivid images, poignant lines, and engaging scenes enter their readers' minds through the senses. At Bennington Writers' Conference, George Garrett instructed our writers' group that we should often begin a story with the sense of smell. In contrast, my friend Elizabeth says, "I remember sounds. I remember the sound of the screen door slamming down at Ma-Ma's in Benevolence, Georgia."

Seeing and hearing, however, are the senses most often used in writing and are overused. The senses of taste, smell, and touch are more stimulating and more effective in reaching readers. We only have to look at advertising on television to understand this idea. Food flashes across the screen continuously. Inside our magazines are attached scented advertisements, "scratch and sniff" samples, and textures to feel.

We all know how a change in seasons and a new scent in the air bring back memories and take us away to another time and place. Marcel Proust (1934), in *Remembrance of Things Past,* shows how one taste, one smell, can bring back a single memory:

I raised to my lips a spoonful of the tea in which I had soaked a
morsel of the cake. No sooner had the warm liquid, and the
crumbs with it, touched my palate than a shudder ran through my
whole body, and I stopped, intent upon the extraordinary changes
that were taking place. An exquisite pleasure had invaded my
senses, but individual, detached, with no suggestion of its origin.
(p. 34)

Throughout the next two pages of Proust's novel, the character tries
to remember why he has this strong response to tea and cake.
Finally, he remembers the tea and cake his Aunt Leonie used to give
him as a boy, "dipping it first in her own cup of real or lime-flower
tea" (1934, p. 36).

Successful writers use these senses because they know how
powerful they are. In a *New Yorker* article, "My Madeleine," Muriel
Spark (2000) refers to Proust's trigger for bringing back memories as
his "Madeleine." These "memory touchstones," she writes, "are most
often connected with smells. Who is not moved to recall some previous experience by, for instance, a waft of honeysuckle, or the smoky
whiff of a coal fire?" (p. 105) In "The Famine of Bengal," Gita Mehta
(1998) writes,

As hungry peasants flooded into Calcutta in search of work for
food, restaurants did brisk business. One roadside stall offered three
options to its customers: a price to see the food. A higher price to
smell the food. A third price to eat the food. (p. 157)

Writing Where You Are

Famous writers write from their own sense of place. When we
read Flannery O'Connor, we expect to read about the people, cul-
tures, and dialect of central Georgia. Alice Walker, we know, will
take us to the little town of Eatonton, Georgia, and to a time when
discrimination was a way of life. When we read Louise Erdrich, we
experience the sights and and hear the sounds of the Native Americans

*I love food. Food movies,
food novels, food just-
about-anything. Love
cookbooks. Like every-
thing about cooking,
including the shopping,
the peeling, the slicing,
the colors, the smells. I
pop open a pod of garlic
with a small cheap knife
I love, and when the
smell drifts up, I'm in
sensory bliss.*

—Beverly Lowry,
"Entrée Nous," We Are What
We Ate, p. 126

in the West. Lee Smith takes us to the Appalachian South. Zora Neale Hurston takes us to the African-American town of Eatonville, Florida, where we learn to read her fluid dialect. Judith Ortiz Cofer takes us between the culture of her grandmother in Puerto Rico and her own life with her mother in Paterson, New Jersey.

The vegetation, the architecture, the birds in the air, the animals on the ground, the temperature and the humidity; the food people eat and the way it is prepared, the sound of voices on the street, the way people pronounce their words—all come from the unique voice of a particular writer's region. And, following the old adage, "write what you know," we know that most famous writers write their best when writing from their own locale.

Writing from Memory

Practicing writers write from their memory. The family stories they listened to at the feet of older family and friends are a great resource and inspiration for many writers. The stories told at the dinner table, the events recalled and triggered by adult happenings, and the happy and painful details that fill our great literature come straight from the memories and lives of our writers.

Following the Directions

All writers follow directions. They know which tactics work and which ones don't. They adhere to certain tried and proven rules. In a short story, for example, something must happen. Most stories and poems must be revised many times before they can be considered finished. Language should be fresh and original, not trite and overused. Novels should contain well-rounded characters who are interesting and who experience change. Writing should contain suspense and conflict. Yes, writers follow directions. But, because they are writers, they take great liberties! When they write from memory, they bend it and stretch it and expand it beyond its original boundaries. In being creative, they add their own special slant, their original writer's voice, their own distinctive view of the world. These

A writer's resource is his or her individuality. We all share a common humanity, and we're also infinitely various. The fiction writer hopes to articulate exactly that singularity of experience where each one of us sees, touches, smells, hears, tastes, thinks, and feels in configurations that are unlike those of everybody else. John Dewey must have had storywriters in mind when he said, "The local is the only universal." Write the story of the blizzard from the point of view of the single snowflake.

—David Huddle,
Writers Ask, *p. 2*

four characteristics of writers—appealing to the senses, writing from one's own locale, writing from memory, and following directions—exist. But they do not exist separate and distinct from one another. Each locale contains its own taste, smell, and texture. Each memory is bathed in locale and senses. And all liberties taken as deviations from the rules are woven tightly together with sense, place, and memory so that they cannot be separated any more easily than the yolk from the white in a beaten egg. These are the tightly woven characteristics of real writing that can be given to our students who write in school.

In this book, these four characteristics of writing are not separated into individual chapters, nor is there a separate list of steps to follow for teaching students these writing qualities. Instead, Chapter 1 reminds us of how everyone learns (and relearns) to write. Chapter 2 sets the stage for successful classroom writing. Chapters 3 through 5 emphasize the writing process. Chapter 6 builds on many of the techniques already presented and shows ways to have fun with writing in the classroom. Chapter 7 relates the ideas given in the book to the institution that both teachers and students must answer to. In Chapter 8, the secret ingredients for teaching writing are revealed.

The four characteristics successful writers use are woven throughout the book in much the same way that they are infused in a writer's mind. A writer doesn't consciously say, "Today I'm going to write from memory," or "Today I shall appeal to the senses." In this book, however, the four characteristics are overtly used to present a writing program. For example, you will find in Chapter 3 activities for appealing to the senses; in Chapter 4, writing with mind pictures; and in Chapter 7, writing a class essay with the senses. Students work specifically with writing from a sense of place in place writing and crime digest activities in Chapter 3 and while working on an essay about our town in Chapter 7. Writing from memory activities include the church story and scars assignment in Chapter 3, the childhood

When I visited my Grandmother Long in the mountains of north Georgia, it was like going back to an earlier time. Her fried apple pies were made from apples she'd raised and then dried. She served them on all occasions: family dinners, church dinners-on-the-ground, food offerings to bereaved families.

—Faye Gibbons,
Writers in the Kitchen,
p. 208

memory story in Chapter 4, and the essay from memory research in Chapter 7. Finally, you will find activities for following directions in Chapters 3 through 5, where you learn the writing process itself, and the steps for making school writing real in Chapter 7.

My Mother's Recipes

Can you imagine how it would be if we learned to walk or talk by having to learn a formula or follow a set of prescribed directions? According to Goldberg (1991a),

> When you bake a cake, you have ingredients: sugar, flour, butter, baking soda, eggs, milk. You put them in a bowl and mix them up, but this does not make a cake. This makes goop. You have to put them in the oven and add heat or energy to transform it into cake, and the cake looks nothing like its original ingredients. . . . In a sense this is what writing is like. You have all these ingredients, the details of your life, but just to list them is not enough. (p. 45)

At the beginning of each chapter of this book, I present a recipe. These recipes are my mother's; they are metaphors for those characteristics of writing that our students need to learn in school. These recipes are part of my memory, and they are particular to my locale. They carry with them stories connected to my childhood. Each recipe, accompanied by a story, a childhood memory, or a secret ingredient, appeals to the sense of taste, smell, and texture.

Each recipe is, as are all recipes, a list of directions to be followed. My mother, however, said that recipes are meant to be "doctored on." I've included her special secret changes to the recipes. These changes, too, are part of the metaphor for what writers do when following writing rules. In essence, what would have been steps to follow from a page in a cookbook or off the side of the can of Crisco shortening, or what would have been a list in a schoolbook or a writing formula to follow, becomes unique in the hands

We were known to eat our pie right on the same plate as our turnip greens so as not to mess up another dish. It didn't matter if the peach cobbler oozed all over the turnip-green juice and the pork grease. "It all goes to the same place," Mama said.

—Bobbie Ann Mason,
"The Burden of the Feast,"
p. 139

of each individual chef or writer. And when we change the recipes to suit ourselves, students and writing teachers can once again say that writing in school is both fun and rewarding.

Recipes and Lesson Plans

Teachers are always alert for new teaching ideas. We go to workshops as attendees and presenters. We greedily grab everything we can find, anything to make our teaching better. Sometimes people say to me, "May I steal your idea?"

"Of course!" I say. "Where do you think I got it?" We go to workshops to learn from one another, and we use what we learn in our classes.

It's the same with cooks and recipes. Good cooks get recipes from wherever they can find them—off shortening cans, from friends and family members, from the side of a cereal box, cut from magazines and newspapers, out of church cookbooks, or simply by word of mouth, passed down through generations. In many cases, cooks don't know where they got a recipe. It just seems that they've always had it.

Many of my lesson plans are my original plans. But I'm sure that many others are picked up here and there at workshops and from colleagues. Some of these ideas I've been using so long in my classes that I don't know where I got the ideas. Others started out as an idea I lifted from somewhere, and then I changed it and made it unique. In this book, I try to give credit where credit is due.

It's the same way with my mother's recipes. The recipes in this book are those I remember from my mother's kitchen. I have searched through her recipe box and found many recipes, some handwritten and others clipped from newspapers and then altered over the years. Others I just wrote down as she made them in her kitchen in front of me. Like lesson plans, I'm sure her recipes are a collection of things begged, borrowed, and shared over the years. Again, I try to give credit where credit is due.

When my mother died a few years ago, I inherited her recipe box. I sat down and read it like a novel—for, in fact, our recipes tell everything about us: where we live, what we value, how we spend our time. Fat content was not a consideration. Biscuits called for lard, and chocolate velvet cake required one cup of mayonnaise.

—Lee Smith,
"Lady Food," We Are What We Ate, p. 202

In no case, either with lesson plans or recipes, do I intentionally take credit for, or give my mother credit for, something that belongs to someone else. Both my lesson plans and my mother's recipes are collections of memory and years of notes. And wherever memory is faulty, please know that every effort has been made to acknowledge the sources fairly.

Teachers as Writers

When we enter a classroom, we cannot leave behind our own lives. To be writing teachers, we must share with students our childhood memories, our parents, a favorite aunt, a cousin we never could tolerate. We must give these favorite parts of our lives to our students on a silver platter and say to them, "This, my dears, is where your writing comes from. I want you to bring me yours and we shall devour our lives together and spread a table of writing which will enter our readers' ears and noses and mouths and tickle the bottoms of their feet and make them remember their own childhoods." And, yes, we must give our mothers' favorite recipes to our students.

Suggestions for the Teacher

◆ Read this book with an open heart.

◆ Select from among the ingredients offered here and sprinkle liberally in your writing classroom.

◆ Begin immediately, regardless of when in the school year or in your teaching career you are encountering these ideas.

Mama's Nut Cake

4 cups all-purpose flour, sifted

1 teaspoon baking powder

1/2 teaspoon salt

3 1/2 sticks butter or margarine

2 cups sugar

6 eggs

2 1/2 teaspoons vanilla

3/4 to 1 pound candied cherries

3/4 to 1 pound candied pineapple

1 quart nuts (halves and pieces, not chopped)

◆ Preheat oven to 200°. Add baking powder and salt to flour. Sift and set aside.

◆ Cream the butter and sugar. Add two eggs at a time, and beat well each time. Gradually add vanilla and 3 cups of the flour mixture.

◆ In a large bowl, mix the remaining cup of flour with the fruit and nuts to keep them from sticking together. Pour the batter over the fruit mixture and stir until well mixed.

◆ Line the bottom of a 10-inch tube pan with brown paper. Grease and flour. (Option: If you wish to share or give smaller loaves as gifts, try two 9" × 5" × 3" loaf pans or four 7" × 2" × 3" pans.) Add the batter, and press it down firmly with spoon or hands.

◆ Put a shallow pan of water on the lower rack of the oven (underneath the cake). Bake for 3 hours. You may increase the heat to 275° for the last 30 minutes to brown the cake. Cool in pan.

◆ When the cake is cool enough, gently remove it from the pan. If the cake is still warm to the touch, cool it on a rack. When the cake is completely cool, wrap it in a soft cloth and then spread the cloth lightly with vegetable oil. You may sprinkle the cloth lightly with wine and add a piece of apple. (Don't put the apple directly on the cake; place it on the cloth. The oil, wine, and apple will help keep the cake moist.) Store in a cool place.

Understanding the Way We Learn to Write

WHEN I WAS A CHILD, THE NUTS IN MAMA'S NUT CAKE WERE THE PECANS THAT FELL from five huge pecan trees that grew around our house. I grew up with those pecan trees, and much of my childhood is connected with them. When my favorite mimosa tree died in the front yard, I learned to climb the pecan trees. From the tops of the tall pecan trees, I could see farther than when I climbed the lower-to-the-ground and safer mimosa limbs. Each fall, the lime-green jackets opened up and released the pecans, letting them fall to the ground. My sister Linda and I picked up the nuts and dropped them into little metal sand buckets, receiving five cents a bucket from our daddy. From inside the house during pecan season, we heard the squirrels running across the roof and dropping shells as they scampered from tree to tree. In autumn, the fallen pecan leaves made huge brown crunchy mounds to dive into.

Pecans were part of our continuing lives, as we'd spend hours sitting on the back porch cracking and picking out nuts. Truman Capote (1996) describes a similar experience: "Three hours later we are back in the kitchen hulling a heaping buggyload of windfall pecans. Our backs hurt from gathering them: how hard they were to find . . . among the concealing leaves, the frosted, deceiving grass" (p. 6).

This recipe, like many others in this book, contains pecans. And like the other recipes to follow, this recipe is connected with childhood memories of my own as well as references in literature. Recipes, like successful writing, mean following directions, appealing to the senses, appreciating one's own unique place, and remembering childhood.

Reluctant to Write

Many students are reluctant writers. We all know them. They are the ones who frown and move slowly when we say it's time for writing. They are the ones who say, "I don't have anything to write about," "I'm not going to do it," "This is boring," or "This is stupid." Perhaps those pecan trees were like reluctant writers—both eager and reluctant to give us their bounty. While the trees eagerly dropped their pecans for us, they showed their reluctance by making us work so hard to crack open their shells and pick out their beautiful meat.

Many of you are reading this book because you have reluctant writers in your classroom. But let's think together for a minute about what makes human beings reluctant to do anything, not just to write. When I think about my own reluctances, the first thing that comes to mind is math. I can sit at home on my sofa with my lapboard and balance my checkbook just fine. But doing math in a classroom with other students, a teacher, and a deadline is a different story. When my 7th grade teacher said, "As soon as you finish this problem, you can go to lunch," I knew I might not get lunch that day. And when I was sent to the chalkboard to work a problem in front of everyone, I knew I was likely to get it wrong and be embarrassed. Often the teacher would tell me to sit down, and I would walk, red-faced, back to my seat.

Sometimes what comes across as reluctance might not be reluctance at all. In the 8th grade I was like a little fish in the water at our lake. But when I took a swimming class in school, my teacher thought I was lazy, or didn't want to get my hair wet, or didn't want to dress out. My problem, however, was that I didn't want to take my glasses off. Without glasses my eyes cross a little, and I didn't want my classmates to see my crossed eyes. So, I wouldn't swim. My teacher labeled me a reluctant swimmer, and no one knew the real reason but me.

Many adults are reluctant writers, often because of the way they were taught to write. They have memories of a paper they slaved over being held up by the teacher as an example of what *not* to do or of getting back a beloved paper covered with red marks. Writing wasn't taught then the way it is now, beginning in the early grades; often students didn't write until high school, and the teacher's response seemed merely an opportunity to point out what was wrong. No wonder many adults are reluctant writers.

Besides writing, think for a minute about what actions in your life give you that feeling of reluctance. Can you figure out what makes you feel that way? How does that reluctance look on you, and how does it feel? How do other people respond to your reluctance? As you teach the writers in your classroom, try to remember your own school experiences with writing. Try to remember yourself as you were in the grade that you now teach. How did you look? What was your classroom like? Where did you sit in that classroom? Who was your teacher, and how did you feel about school? What things in your life then gave you that feeling of reluctance? Was writing one of them?

How We Learn to Write

I have learned a great deal about the teaching of writing by studying how young children first learn to write. As a teacher for more than 30 years and as a writer attending workshops, I have studied the writing of both adults and children, and the writing of both gifted and at-risk students. Through these experiences, I have come to believe that we all learn to write the same way. Regardless of our age or our ability, we need to begin at the same place and move through the same stages as we learn to write. From kindergarten

Our original family home no longer stands. The old wood-burning cookstove has rusted into pieces. The silver teas are a thing of the past. But precious recipes are still intact, and the tastes and smells of the foods of my childhood let me know that I can go back again.

—Dori Sanders,
Dori Sanders' Country Cooking, *pp. IX–XV*

students to established authors teaching at conferences, we all learn through the same process. Let me show you what I mean.

The Continuum

As you read this book, regardless of the grade level you teach, it will be helpful to think of the individual students in your classroom as being at some point along a continuum in their writing ability. Instead of thinking of your students as all on the same grade level in writing, think of one classroom as containing many different levels.

Just think about it—we have no trouble thinking of the teaching of reading in this way. In using individual computer-based reading programs with my 9th grade students, I determine my students' reading abilities. In one 9th grade classroom, the reading scores may range from as low as 2nd grade to as high as the first year in college. Likewise, one classroom of diverse students contains many different writing levels.

Early Writing Development

Young children learn to write in predictable stages. Understanding these early stages can help teachers become better writing teachers for all ages of students.

Prekindergarten and Kindergarten Writing

Drawing is the way young children first begin to write. The prekindergarten writing in Figure 1.1 (p. 6) is sometimes referred to as "nonrepresentational" for obvious reasons. It doesn't seem to represent anything. It may look like drawing or scribbling to us, but to the preK child, it is writing. If we approach a preK child, point to the drawing, and say, "Tell me about your story," the child won't even give us a puzzled look, for this is the preK child's way of writing.

Marjorie Frank (1995) writes about prekindergarten and kindergarten children, "Since your writers are too young to write lengthy pieces (or to write at all), the time is free for spreading excitement

It is not children but adults who have separated writing from art, song, and play; it is adults who have turned writing into an exercise on lined paper, into a matter of rules, lessons, and cautious behavior. . . . We, as adults, may not believe in writing for preschool children—but the children believe in it.

—Lucy Calkins,
The Art of Teaching Writing, p. 59

about words, showing off the talent of language, and making communication easy and enjoyable" (pp. 200–201). She gives the following suggestions for use with these very young writers:

◆ Sensitize them to their environment by getting them to experience things with their five senses.

◆ Talk about ideas and discoveries.

◆ Tape-record answers to questions.

◆ Listen to songs.

◆ Read!

◆ Compose orally.

◆ Invite volunteers to take dictation.

◆ Show off writing.

◆ Pair with an older child to write together.

◆ Emphasize short pieces, such as riddles and word collections.

Most important, let prekindergarten children act like writers. Writing starts with drawing. What looks like a nonrepresentational scribble to an adult (Figure 1.1) is a picture with a story to its young author. From there, writers often progress to the kindergarten writing in Figure 1.2 (p. 6), which is nonrepresentational plus words. The kindergarten writing in Figure 1.2 is actually an entire story with a beginning, middle, and end. The drawing is the beginning and the middle; the ending is, "And they all died." It is a sad story, but a story just the same. In Figure 1.3 (p. 6), the kindergarten drawing is representational, and the words label the picture a "crystal palace." Figure 1.4 (p. 6) shows how young writers often display letters at random. As the writers gain experience and knowledge, words and sentences emerge clearly. The drawing in Figure 1.5 (p. 7) is a story that says "A little girl is ice-skating. She is four on a sunny day."

A kindergarten teacher may illustrate that there are many ways of writing by displaying samples of various kinds of kindergarten writing around the classroom. By using this ever-present reminder, the teacher conveys to students that no one way of writing is better or worse than another; they are just all different.

Figure 1.1
NONREPRESENTATIONAL WRITING

—prekindergarten

Figure 1.2
NONREPRESENTATIONAL WRITING AND WORDS

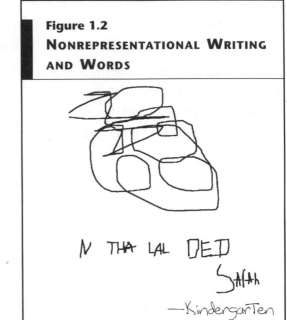

N THA LAL DED

Sarah

—Kindergarten

Figure 1.3
REPRESENTATIONAL WRITING PLUS WORDS

Kristl PaLs

Ryan

—Kindergarten

Figure 1.4
RANDOM LETTERS, LEFT TO RIGHT

—Kindergarten

Figure 1.5
WORDS AND SENTENCES

A little girl is ice-skating. She is four On a sunny day.

—Kindergarten

1st Grade Through 3rd Grade Writing

Consider the writing samples in Figures 1.6 through 1.11 from 1st through 3rd graders. Note especially the two samples from 3rd grade classmates (Figures 1.10 and 1.11, p. 9). These two writers are obviously on different levels—one, in the earlier stages of printing and illustrating and writing short, simple sentences; the other, writing with more detailed development and varied sentence structure.

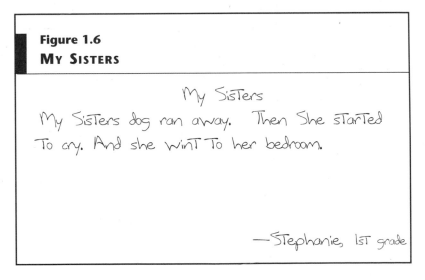

Figure 1.6
MY SISTERS

My Sisters
My Sisters dog ran away. Then She sTarTed To cry. And she winT To her bedroom.

—STephanie, 1sT grade

As you can see, these samples are all different, and the grade levels merge and cross one another.

Figure 1.7
RESOLUTION

my resolution for The
new year is To be Good To
my mom an oTher
and don'T jump in my shoes
and do my work
and giT To school on Time
and don'T play wiTh bad boy.
I will be good To My Teacher
and sTop being bad in school

—1sT grade

Figure 1.8
BEING A TEACHER

I would like To Be like Mrs.
Hawkin Becalls I coud Tell
The class wuT To bo.
I miT geT Tiyerd of Be a
Techer Becalls I will geT
agervaTid.

—2nd grade

Figure 1.9
A GOOD JOB

If I were a Teacher, I would serve children and I would pass ouT
paper. I would leT my class draw picTures if They are good. A
Teacher is a good job because iT looks fun To be a Teacher. And I
would have fun being one. I hope I will be a Teacher some day.

—2nd grade

Figure 1.10
LEAVES

Once I saw leaves in my yard. I sTarTed To pick Them up. Then my sisTer came ouT To help me. We goT a bag To make iT easier.

—3rd grade

Figure 1.11
BOY SCOUTS

Boy ScouTs

The boy scouTs followed The Tracks To a cave. We found a hole in a mouTain. Are den ledder wend down iT. There was skulls and gold loTs of gold. There was a loT of gold. We Took a bunch ouT buT There was loTs more. We Took iT ouT and wenT To The bus. The gold was gone we Took all of iT. Now we wenT farTher in The cave. There was more and more skulls. iT was dark and dap. Suddenly Andrew found a Teasure chesT. When we wenT farTher Byron found anoTher one. Now we were all Timbling wiTh are rubyres. Suddenly a skull fell we all scred. We ran as fasT as we could one afTer anoTher droping all The pearls and plases sTones. We sTarTed an avalanch in The cave. We losT all of are sTuff. We ThoughT we had some gold, buT we lefT The door open and iT goT sToled.

—3rd grade

4th and 5th Grade Writing

Look at the samples in Figures 1.12 through 1.16 (pp. 12–15) from 4th and 5th graders. Not only are these samples different from one another, but at this point I can tell little difference between this writing and some of the writing by 9th graders. As soon as children learn to write, the lines between the grades begin to blur. If we put students from grades 3 through 10 in one classroom, some students would print and some would write in cursive; some would write long, well-developed sentences, and some would write fragments. Some would use large mature vocabularies while others would use only short words that they were sure they could spell. And the students' real grade levels would not be the deciding factor. A helpful book for studying the way children learn to write is Naomi Gordon's (1984) *Classroom Experiences: The Writing Process in Action.*

The Way We Best Learn to Write

To write successfully, students—and all of us—need to begin with personal writing for self. Writing for self means loosening up: freewriting; journal keeping; and concrete, self-centered writing. Compare writing at this stage with toddlers who are first learning to talk. As young children play, they seem self-centered, talking to themselves, shutting others out. James Moffett (1966) writes,

> This is the first discourse of the child, who does not distinguish between speaking to himself and speaking to another. . . . According to the great psychologist of child development, Jean Piaget, who has called this discourse "egocentric speech," the very young child thinks aloud, talks to the air, not expecting others to pay attention or respond to what he says; his talk is an accompaniment to whatever he is doing at the moment. (p. 569)

So it is with the personal, beginning stage of writing.

"The great blessing we all have is that, according to the scientists, our most enduring memories are taste and smell. I believe this. I can still taste the snickerdoodles that we got for a snack in kindergarten . . . "

—David Haynes,

"Chinese Spareribs," We Are What We Ate, p. 122

The next step in writing is to reach out to others. Often writing during this stage is characterized by letters and notes written to a perceived audience—friends, parents, teachers—from whom a response is anticipated. As this stage progresses, the writer becomes more aware of his audience. This writing period parallels the talking stage in which children ask lots of questions to learn how to communicate with others. The writer is close to the reading audience at this stage. Moffett (1966) describes this stage as follows: "*You* is born from the rib of *I* in the form of a listener who is actually another person." This is the second stage of speech, "which Piaget calls 'socialized' because the speaker adapts his discourse to a second person whom he wishes to influence and by whom he is willing to be influenced" (p. 570).

And only last should students learn to write expository, more abstract kinds of writing, including persuasive essays, newspaper articles, or research papers. In this third stage, the most distant audience from self, the writer is more concerned with a relationship with a *subject*. Learning to write, Moffett (1966) says, "is a matter of 'de-centering,' of breaking through our egocentricity to new points of view. . . . We achieve decentering by adapting ourselves to things and people outside ourselves" (p. 572).

In each of the stages we are, as Moffett (1966) writes, "increasing the distance between the speaker and his listener, between the speaker and his subject. Thus, the central concept is the trinity of first, second, and third persons—*I, you,* and *he*" (p. XII).

Beginning writing, at its up close and personal best, should be pleasant. As Natalie Goldberg (1991a) writes,

In Judaism there is an old tradition that when a young boy first begins to study, the very first time, after he reads his first word in the Torah, he is given a taste of honey or a sweet. This is so he will always associate learning with sweetness. It should be the same with writing. Right from the beginning, know it is good and pleasant. (p. 110)

Figure 1.12
GHOST STORY

"The Ghost That Got Scared"

Once I was walking near a graveyard. I went in and saw a ghosts. I ran out of the graveyard and the ghost followed me. I turned around and said, "Boo!" The ghost didn't get scared. So I got behind a bush, and when he came by I jumped up and said "Boo!" He went into the graveyard and got more ghost. I got behind the bush again and said "Get off my land." Then I jumped up and said "Boo!" They all got scared and ran back in the graveyard. When I started to leave one of them said "Excuse me, I would like to be your friend." I said "OK." I played with him everytime I went to that graveyard.

—4th grade

Unfortunately, the increased emphasis on testing has pushed many teachers, even as early as 2nd grade teachers, to begin teaching expository writing in formulas, such as the hamburger paragraph (the "meat" of the paragraph is placed between the "buns" of an introduction and conclusion) or the five-paragraph theme (three middle paragraphs flanked by an introduction and conclusion; see Chapter 7 for more information). If teachers insist on these forms too soon or too exclusively, students miss the chance to learn to write the way they learn best—by beginning with personal writing. In contrast, if they begin with personal writing and become fluent during these early stages, they later write better expository writing.

Figure 1.13
BALLOONS

The Balloon Lifting Experience

One Time Justin, Chris, John, and Joseph went To a fair. They were going on all The rides. And riding many Times. Every-Time They went on a ride They got Two balloons. PreTTy soon They had so many balloons ThaT They weren'T allowed on any rides. So They mad an angrement ThaT one of Them would hold all of The balloons while The oThers went on rides. They picked JusTin To be The firsT one. So They handed him all Their balloons. BuT before They could go anywhere JusTin sTarTed floaTing away. Chris grabed JusTin buT iT was no use They boTh sTarTed floaT-ing away. John grabed Chris buT sTill noT enough weighT. So Joseph grabed John buT sTill There wasn'T enough waiT To hold all The balloons down. And They all sTarTed floaTing away. BuT Their fairy god moThers helped Them. Their balloons goT caughT on a lighT pole and They were able To climb down.
　　　The End

　　　　　　　　　　　　　　　　　　　　　　　　—4Th grade

Learning Through Making Mistakes

　　As children first learn to talk, they make mistakes that adults think are cute—saying *basketti,* for example, when they mean *spaghetti,* or *wa-wa* for water. Yet, when children use these same experimentations in their writing, we often say they are wrong, and we correct them. We need to admire and appreciate all the steps beginning writers go through, for these stages are truly unique,

Figure 1.14
MARS

My Trip To Mars

Once upon a Time not long ago my dad planned a special Trip To Mars. We got in To a rocket and Flew into space. We saw lots of stars and comics. Then when we got into The deep part of space our ship started bumped by some kind of force. I looked outside and saw a big giant rock coming Towards us. Then when iT was abouT To hiT us I said duck and everyone did. Then a rock came righT Trough.

—5Th grade

Figure 1.15
WEDDING

My Mom's Wedding Party

One day my mom got married. AfTer The wedding They had a very weird wedding party. My mom and my dad had The party aT Their new house on The lake. My mom loves pizza, so They had pizza and cake mostly. My mom just saT and aTe a loT. Then she was getTing another piece of pizza, when she Tripped. The pizza wenT flying, and iT landed on The cake. Then my mom said, "I always wanTed a pizza cake."

—5Th grade

Figure 1.16
CHIMPANZEE STORY

The Life of Me: A Chimpanzee

One day I was out in The woods. IT was a beautiful day and I
was picking flowers. Suddenly I heard The noise of The bushes
moving. I stood still. Then The woods became dark and eerie. The
sound kept coming closer. Suddenly a witch jumped out. She was
a mean witch and she wore black clothes. She held her arms out
To me and Poosh! My flowers flew everywhere. I heard The
witch say Ha, Ha, Ha! Then she was gone. I was scared. I
began To run but I Tripped over my arms. I got up and looked aT
myself. My arms were brown, furry, and long. My whole body
was bornwn. I was short. I felt for my hair but I . . .

—5Th grade

interesting, and entertaining. In addition, writers of all ages need to return again and again to these important beginning stages of writing for self and of being allowed to make mistakes as thoughts take shape.

The Continuum: A Reminder

Again, as you read this book, please think of your individual students as somewhere along the continuum of writing levels in the same way we think of reading levels. From kindergarten to adult, writers are writers. Good writing is good writing, regardless of age or ability level. If it is successful, we are interested in it, we are entertained by it, and we learn something from it. Writing is a way we can all come together, for, when it comes to writing, we have every-thing in common. In Chapter 2, you will begin to learn ways to set up the best atmosphere for a writing classroom.

Suggestions for the Teacher

◆ Share with your students the actions you feel reluctant about, even those times when you were a reluctant writer. Write together about these things and put samples up on the wall to show students that adults can feel reluctant and that it's okay!

◆ Post different styles of writing around the room, including your own.

◆ Display a photograph of yourself when you were about the age of your students and tell them about some of your school experiences.

◆ Locate yourself on the writing continuum. As a writer, based on the development stages in this chapter, what is your level?

Mama's Pecan Pie

3 beaten eggs

1/2 cup sugar

1 tablespoon flour

1/4 teaspoon salt

1/2 cup light corn syrup

1/2 cup dark corn syrup

1/4 cup melted butter

1 1/2 teaspoons vanilla

1 cup whole pecan halves

1 deep-dish, 9-inch pie shell, either frozen or your favorite recipe

◆ Preheat the oven to 375°. Beat the eggs. In a separate bowl, combine the sugar, flour, and salt. Add the dry mixture to the eggs. Mix in light and dark corn syrup, melted butter (cooled), and vanilla.

◆ Place half of the pecans in the bottom of the crust, slowly pour the filling mixture onto crust, and then add the remainder of the pecans to the top.

◆ Bake for 40 to 45 minutes or until pie is firm. If the crust gets too brown, place foil around the edge, or lower the oven temperature a few degrees.

Getting the Classroom Atmosphere Right for Writing

2

EVERY YEAR ON MY BIRTHDAY, MY MOTHER BAKED ME A PECAN PIE. SHE PUT A candle in the center and, even after I was grown and had moved out of the house, she had me over and came walking into the room, the lit candle shining in her eyes as she sang "Happy Birthday." Later that evening at home, I savored more of that pie, nibbling around the edges, breaking off pieces of crust, eating the toasted pecans off the top one by one, spooning up the filling, and making that birthday feeling last as long as I could. Over the next few days, I eventually ate the whole pie, all by myself.

But there was more to that pie than the sweetness and the toasted nuts. There was the love, the gift from my mother to me. That pie stood for something. The pie tasted like my mother's love.

I have many memories of being nurtured in the classroom by my teachers. One, in particular, has a direct connection with food. In the 3rd grade, in Mrs. Rogers's class, we used to have spelling bees. I almost always won the spelling bee, except for the times that Stan Puckett or Becky McKnight beat me. When I won, Mrs. Rogers would go to her desk drawer and take out a little glass jar filled with candy. It was always the same kind of candy, the creamy melt-in-your-mouth kind similar to candy corn. There were two choices, an orange and a chocolate, and I got to have one of each. I remember

In my mind I would roll out mud circles, and more daintily in thought than ever in fact I would tuck these crusts in pans. In my mind's eye I would see myself, in passionate imitation of adult pie-makers, layering in flowers or pebbles, dribbling over them my sandbox sand for sugar, and adding danks of wet mud butter. Then, carefully, with an enormous sigh of satisfaction that comes as one nears a task's completion, I spread a top crust over my pie's filling, and with the stubby dimpled fingers I see now in my photographs at that age, I pinched together, around the pie's entire circumference, the edges of the top and bottom mud crusts. What was in the pie was a secret only I knew.

—Judith Moore,
Never Eat Your Heart Out,
p. 3–4

sitting at my desk, letting that candy dissolve slowly in my mouth, and relishing that satisfying feeling of winning. That candy meant that I was good at something, that my teacher liked me, and that I was being rewarded.

Once when I was sharing memories of early school years with a teacher friend, I asked her who her favorite teacher was. She remembered her 4th grade teacher. Why? My friend was entrusted with going to the teacher's house next door and turning on the oven so dinner would be ready when the teacher went home. Her feelings for this teacher were entwined with the trust the teacher gave her—and the feelings are connected with the actions. No child would get a kick out of going to turn on an oven. But the teacher trusted her and, in turn, my friend liked, even loved, her. That's how it felt.

No classroom can be complete or successful without positive feelings and encouragement. Lucy Calkins (1994) writes, "I began to believe that my goal in life isn't to lure young people to care about writing; it's to lure them to care about something" (p. 172). Classroom atmosphere is the first, most important part of teaching writing. It is that thing that students see and feel in their surroundings as they walk into your classroom; atmosphere affects students from the first time you look into their faces. How students feel in your classroom and how students feel about themselves in your classroom is powerfully influenced by atmosphere. This chapter contains ideas for establishing a classroom atmosphere that is conducive to teaching writing. The ideas address various aspects of the classroom, including the physical appearance of the classroom, getting-to-know-you techniques, daily self-esteem raisers, and other reliable classroom practices.

Naturally, some golden moments can't be planned. Once I went to the National Council of Teachers of English conference in Detroit and brought home a gold pen I picked up from a publisher's display. Back at school a few days later, a student standing by my desk admired the pen I was using. On the spur of the moment, I handed the pen to him and said, "This is your hard-working pen. There is more to this pen than a pen. It is a symbol for my belief in your ability to succeed." For weeks, that student wrote his little heart out with that gold pen. Serendipitous occasions don't happen daily, but every day you can help students believe that they can succeed.

Classroom Atmosphere

I am cute.
I am lovable.
I am handsome.
I am wonderful.
I am excellent.
I am fantastic.
I am worthy.
I am a friendly person.
I am a powerful person.
I am a responsible person.
I am lying about everything.
—Kelvin, 9th grade

Once the pie is brought to the table, I like to take a moment and admire it. I like to give the pie a chance to wet the mouth with anticipation of its tastes (the mouth's imagination at work).

—Judith Moore,
Never Eat Your Heart Out,
p. 12

Creating a classroom atmosphere where students feel comfortable exploring their writing selves, as exemplified in Kelvin's poem, requires your energy and imagination. In this chapter, I introduce many of the ideas that have worked in my writing classrooms over the years. Try a few of these activities right away, introducing the ideas you think will best work with your student population.

Creating an Inviting Space

Much of classroom atmosphere lies in physical surroundings. What children actually see when they enter your classroom has much to do with how they feel while there.

Banners

Using felt and fabric paint, try making colorful banners containing motivational sayings and hang these on the walls of your classroom:

- ◆ I am the most powerful person in my life.
- ◆ Success lies not in being the best but in doing your best.
- ◆ It is okay to fail; it is not okay to give up.
- ◆ I am somebody. I am here for a purpose: I will do something important in my life.

Sweatshirts

Make sweatshirts that prominently display motivational or inspiring themes and wear them to school to keep ideas fresh. Students know that you believe in the words you wear and will infer that you are wearing the words for them.

Music Between Classes

Try playing music between class changes or subject shifts. Keep students guessing as to what the music will be. It could be the Beatles, country music, jazz, or ragtime. Playing music to signify transitions makes your classroom a little different from others and helps students to enter the room in an upbeat mood. Music lifts the teacher's mood, too.

Orphan Papers

Have a special place on the bulletin board with a sign for "orphan papers." Hang papers there that have no name on them, and students will find them. The atmosphere of the classroom is enhanced as students identify their own papers without being fussed at.

Graduation Tape

I have a videotape of the high school graduation with the seniors marching to "Pomp and Circumstance." I play this tape on the first day of school as my students are entering the room. As soon as they sit down, I point to the screen and say, "This is why you are

The dining room was the heart of every old Southern home. Here the family gathered every day, gave thanks to the Lord for his blessings, talked of ancestors and descendants, weddings and christenings, gardens and fields. Life that had happened and life that might happen. Time passed sweetly and unhurriedly. We liked to think that we honored the past, celebrated the present, and took courage for the future.

—Luann Landon, Dinner at Miss Lady's, p. 2

here." I repeat this tape again one or two times during the semester just to remind them. The graduation tape works for young students, too, because everyone is aiming for that goal.

Inviting the Students into Class

Students can think of plenty of reasons not to attend class. One part of creating a positive and welcoming classroom atmosphere is to make class a place they want to be. Let students know you're glad to see them each new day.

Handshakes

Handshakes are an effective way of establishing rapport with your students. Every day, try shaking each student's hand and ask for a good firm businessperson's handshake in return. According to Clare LaMeres (1990), the theory behind this activity is that "You can't be mean to someone you look in the eye every day." Handshakes can do more toward establishing teacher-student rapport than anything else you try.

Large class sizes often prohibit the one-on-one contact students and teachers need. Daily handshakes give us a chance to establish personal contact with every child every day. You will be surprised at how much a hand squeeze and good eye contact can tell you about a student's mood.

Handshakes work beautifully with all grade levels and can start your day just right. The tiny 1st grade hands or the big rough high school football player hands are always reassuring. Even the sophisticated advanced placement students warm to the handshakes. And if you forget, students will always remind you. You could try giving a short class starter activity, like freewriting, at the beginning of the period and then shake hands as you take up the papers. Other ways would be to stand at the door and greet students as they come in (you may give them the option of giving you a high-five instead). Or, you might shake hands as the students leave and wish them a good day. Clare LaMeres (1990) says to students as they leave, "Make a great future!"

Don't wait until the beginning of a school year to try this strategy. Start tomorrow. Just tell your students, "I'm reading a book that gave me this idea, and I want us to try it." Even the spontaneity shows students that you, the teacher, are always learning new things and are courageous and adventuresome enough to try them. After all, kids like crazy teachers. If you can establish a reputation of being eccentric, you can get away with anything!

Standing Ovations

Similar to the handshakes in effectiveness, standing ovations are another wonderful idea from LaMeres. Every day one student gets a standing ovation. If a student has a birthday that day, that student gets the standing ovation. If there are no birthdays, just pull a card from a stack of index cards prepared with students' names. When a student is identified as the standing ovation for the day, he moves to the center of the room, reads aloud a saying or famous quotation (from a banner or from an available book or list of quotations), and then everyone stands and applauds.

Teach students from the very beginning the reason for the standing ovation: We are all put on this earth for a purpose, and in this life we have a job to do that no one can do as well as we can. This makes each and every one of us important, indispensable, and powerful. When we give our students and peers a standing ovation, we are recognizing their essential worth—and that's something worth celebrating!

Songs

Some of the ideas I suggest for establishing classroom atmosphere may not feel natural to your teaching style, and if this is true, then just throw them out the window. But, if it feels right to you, try having students learn to sing with you. Choose songs with motivational lyrics and uplifting words. High school students may learn their alma mater to sing at graduation—and there's nothing wrong with teaching it to 9th graders to promote pride and school spirit while enhancing classroom atmosphere. The song will serve to remind students that they are preparing for their graduation. Younger children may learn a school song or a graduation song for their grade level. You can imagine the pride I feel at graduation when I see my former 9th graders in their caps and gowns—and I enjoy knowing that they are probably the only members of the graduating class who didn't have to learn the alma mater just in time for graduation.

Student Experts

We have student experts of all kinds in our classrooms. Some students are good at spelling; some are good monitors for computerized reading tests; some are able to help other students boot up the computer; and some are excellent proofreaders. Saving the plastic pin-backed nametags from conferences and replacing your name with an expert label is an excellent way to identify students as expert of the day, such as Proofreading Expert.

Certificates

Give homemade computer certificates for everything—highest grade on a daily quiz, fewest tardies, most creative poem, best attendance. Make a big production out of presenting a certificate: call the student to the front and make the announcement, followed by applause and cheering. Certificates are all about celebrating the good things that happen in class. A sample certificate is included in Figure 2.1 (p. 26).

A Time for Talking

Students are going to talk to one another, right? If we try to keep them from talking, they are going to talk out of turn. But, if every 10 or 15 minutes we create a time for them to talk to one another about what we want them to talk about, then talking won't be so much of a problem. For example, if you are reading a story in literature, tell students to turn to their neighbor and predict what is going to happen next, or analyze a character's actions, or make up a different ending. Give them a definite period of time, and set a

It was hard to believe that she had not been in that kitchen for years; she was so much a part of it. She put the crocks away with a sure, precise touch, moving leisurely and ample from the stove to the dresser, looking into the pantry and the larder as though there were not an unfamiliar corner. When she had finished, everything in the kitchen had become part of a series of patterns.

—Katherine Mansfield, "Prelude," *Stories, p. 70*

Figure 2.1
CERTIFICATE OF ACHIEVEMENT

Certificate of Achievement
Awarded to

_____

In recognition of outstanding
performance, exceptional achievement,
and downright good work

In _____

This _____ *day of* _____ , *20* ___

From _____

timer for about two minutes. At the end of that time, use a signal—
either the chime like those for the time or a little bell kept at a check-
out counter in a store (you can get them at an office supply store for
a few dollars). By scheduling talking, you are choosing the topic.

Talking, by the way, is a human expression, not just a student's
vice. We like to communicate with one another. If you don't believe
this, just see how long it takes the principal to get the attention of
staff at the next faculty meeting.

Laugh with Them

Students do hilarious things in the classroom. And what do we do? We frown and point our finger and express displeasure. Then we go down to the faculty lounge, tell the other teachers what happened, and we all die laughing. We need to let the students see us laugh; we need to laugh with them with a good out-loud belly laugh. High school students often come in the room in a bad mood. It may be something serious, or it may just be bad hair day. I have a can of vanilla air freshener in my classroom, labelled Bad Mood Spray. If a student comes into the room grumping and complaining, I pick up the can, spray high in the air, and say "Uh, oh! Bad mood! Bad mood!" This action turns a potential class poisoner into a cause for laughter. If any students have asthma or allergies, just pretend to spray by holding the can up and saying "P-s-s-s-t! Uh, oh! Bad mood!" Students also have the right to remind me: "Looks like Ms. Worsham needs the bad mood spray today!"

Involving the Parents

A note from a teacher to a parent doesn't have to be bad news. Letting parents know how well a child is doing in class invites them to be involved in the child's education. Parents who know what their child is learning in school are more likely to reinforce positive lessons at home. Communicate with the parents of your students whenever possible.

Sending Postcards for Good Reasons. Keep bright postcards, perhaps with motivational messages, on hand and mail two or three a day, or however many your schedule will allow, telling parents good, positive things about their child. For example,

Dear Mrs. Roberson, I want you to know how much I am enjoying having Tassie in my English class this semester. She has improved so much in her writing. I especially enjoyed the story she wrote about going fishing with her grandmother. I know you are very proud of her. Sincerely, Mrs. Worsham

---

Patrons of the café got quite a surprise when they read the menu last week that featured, among other things: Fillet of Possum . . . Prime Rib of Polecat . . . Goat's Liver and Onions . . . Bull Frog Pudding and Turkey Buzzard Pie Ala Mode.

An unsuspecting couple, who had come all the way from Gate City for dinner, read the menu and were halfway down the block when Idgie opened the door and yelled April Fool's at them.

—Fannie Flagg,
Fried Green Tomatoes at the Whistle Stop Café, *p. 56*

Parents appreciate positive messages from school. One mother even mentioned her postcard as I went through the drive-in window at the bank. These are the kinds of mailings from the school that a student doesn't throw away before the parent gets home.

Calling Home About Absences. To encourage regular attendance at school, try calling home after a student's absence. Sometimes when I call, the student answers. I say, "Today is your sixth absence. Why aren't you here?" Occasionally the responses I get from these phone calls make me laugh. When Arthur told me his sister forgot to wake him up, I told him to get an alarm clock because it wasn't his sister's responsibility to wake him up. Another time, a parent called the school and left this message with the secretary: "Rodney isn't coming to school today. Please tell Ms. Worsham I already know it!"

Figure 2.2 (p. 29) gives some suggestions for calling parents about their child's behavior and class experiences as well as ways to inform them and enlist their support.

Calling Parents for Good Reasons. I know, I know. We have to spend so much time calling parents for bad reasons that how could we possibly have time to call parents for good reasons? Well, let me tell you, this is one of the most rewarding things you can do for yourself. Besides, it is tremendous fun. This is how it goes:

> Hello, Mrs. Williams? This is Sandra Worsham. I'm Tony's English teacher at Baldwin High School, and I'm calling to let you know how much I'm enjoying having Tony in my class this semester.

Pause. Long pause. And what is Mrs. Williams expecting? The *but,* of course. She's waiting to hear the rest of the story, the real reason I called. So I continue.

> No, really, that's the reason I called. Tony has improved so much, and he comes in the room in a good mood and just adds so much to class.

I don't think you can describe emotion you have not felt. You know, you have to know what it's like—what it is to feel a certain thing—or your description or your use of these emotions will be artificial and shallow.

—*Eudora Welty,*
as quoted in Brans (1984),
p. 297

Figure 2.2
CALLING PARENTS

◆ Take the offensive: "May I speak with Margaret Witherspoon, please?" "Hi, I'm Sandra Worsham, Harold's English teacher at Baldwin High School. I need your help with Harold."

◆ Focus on what the student is learning (or not learning) and less with the trouble he is causing. "I'm afraid Harold is going to get behind. You know, it's hard for students to catch up after they get behind."

◆ Always call parents when a student talks back, if at all possible during the day, before the student gets home that afternoon. Tell the parent exactly what the child said. "I thought you would like for me to let you know the way Harold talked to me today. He told me he was sick of all this ____ from me. I know you don't want Harold talking to his teachers that way, so I wanted to be sure to let you know so you could speak to him for me."

◆ Tell parents what growing up does to some kids. "Sometimes in the ____ grade, children begin to act differently than ever before. Sometimes they get off track at this age. We have a lot of ____ grade failures, and we would like to keep this from happening to Harold."

◆ When you call about absences, be sure the parents understand the school rules about absences and the penalties, and let them know you consider it their responsibility to get the child to school. "This is Harold's sixth absence. You know, if they have more than 10 absences in a class, they lose credit for that class. Harold must be here every day in order to learn and to pass his classes."

◆ End the conversation by asking the parents to tell you how you can do a better job with their child and by telling them you would like to meet them in person. Ask them to come to PTA meetings and open house and to schedule an appointment soon. (Again, you're on the offensive.) "Please let me know if you can think of anything that will help me teach Harold better. And please come up to the school sometime. I would like to have the chance to meet you."

◆ Tell them thank you. Let them know how much you appreciate their help. Do whatever you can to get the parents on your side. Parents are our best allies!

One mother replied, "Praise Jesus!"

These phone calls are especially fun when you call about a student who is often in trouble. Several parents have told me that, though they have received many calls from school over the years, mine was the first *good* call. Can you imagine how it must feel to be a parent, sending a beloved child to school, and only receiving calls for bad reasons?

Special Activities for the First Week

Let students know from the first moment of the first day that your class is going to be different. Replace lectures, drills, and introductions to the syllabus with community-building activities that will bring your class together quickly.

Name Game

It is important to learn students' names as quickly as possible. Here's how you can learn at least all first names within two or three days. This is how it works: Begin on one side of the room and ask a student, "What is your name?"

"Amy," the student may say. Then move to the next student. "What is your name?" you ask

"Benjamin."

"Okay, Benjamin," you say, "What is her name?"

"Amy," Benjamin says.

Then move to the next student. "What is your name?"

"Carmen."

"Carmen, what are their names?"

"Amy and Benjamin."

Keep moving around the room with all names being repeated until the last student has named everyone in the room. As names are repeated, concentrate and say them to yourself.

When the last student has finished, say, "Okay, everybody go sit somewhere else." After "fruit basket turnover," ask students, "Who can name everybody now?" After a couple of days, you will likely remember names even when you see students in the hallway.

An alternative method is to have students think of an adjective, beginning with the same first letter as their first name, that describes them—Amiable Amy, Big Man Benjamin, Charismatic Carmen. This little mnemonic trick helps commit the names to memory.

Meet Your Neighbor or Student of the Week

Have students think of 10 questions they would like to ask someone they are meeting for the first time. These questions may be about hobbies, pets, best and worst subjects, music, and sports. Have students work in pairs and turn their desks to face their partner, toes to toes. Students should take turns interviewing each other by asking the 10 questions and writing the answers. After the interview, ask students to use the information to compose a paragraph with the title of Student of the Week or Meet Your Neighbor. This strategy is good practice for students in gathering information and composing a paragraph. After everyone has finished, ask the students to read their paragraphs aloud. This is a good activity for beginning sharing aloud because everybody is looking at the student being read about rather than at the student who is reading aloud.

Spotlighting

Several activities in this book are almost foolproof. Spotlighting is one of those activities. Using a form called "Interesting and Unusual Things about Me," students write a list of as many facts about themselves as there are people in the room (thus, if you have 14 students, create a sheet with the title at the top and 15 numbered lines). Don't let the words "interesting" and "unusual" confuse them. Just explain that you mean any facts about them.

Give some examples to show them what you mean by facts, such as I raise hamsters; I have been to Russia three times; I eat pizza for breakfast every day; I first learned to roller skate when I was 50 years old.

After everyone has completed a list, give students a new form called "Spotlighting." The form has two numbered columns, one for names and the other for facts. At this point, give students the chance to do the things they love most—get up, move around, and talk to one another! Ask students to trade facts with other students, one at a time, and with the teacher. Be sure students don't just hand

Y'all know we can't invite people to our town just dry long so. I god, naw. We got tuh feed 'em something, and 'tain't nothin' people laks better 'n barbecue. . . . Tell yo' womenfolks tuh do 'round 'bout some pies and cakes and sweet p'tater pone.'
That's the way it went, too. The women got together the sweets and the men looked after the meats.

—Zora Neale Hurston,
Their Eyes Were Watching God, p. 71

over the list to fellow students and say, "Choose one." The idea is to talk to one another and give away a fact and receive one. They write down the name and the fact for each student they talk to, striking off facts as they are given away to avoid repetition.

After completing this phase, students return to their desks. Move a special chair to the center of the room and identify it as the spotlighting chair. Ask each student to sit in the spotlighting chair, one at a time. While a student sits there, the center of attention, the other students take turns saying aloud the things they have learned about that student. Then the student receives applause, and the next student is chosen for the chair.

The spotlighting activity may be lengthened or shortened depending on the amount of time you want to give it. I usually let it take two or three days because it is important to me that students feel comfortable with one another before we begin to write. But if time constraints prevail, work with fewer facts about each student. An elementary student's list of facts is in Figure 2.3 (p. 33).

The spotlighting activity is useful when you begin teaching students how to pass writing tests (see Good Things About Me in Chapter 7). Students should keep this and other writing activities in their writer's notebook (see Chapter 3). One important benefit of the spotlighting activity is the information the teacher learns about students. The more you know about students, the better you will be at helping them think of writing topics.

Here is a three-step summary of the spotlighting procedure:

1. List as many things about you as there are people in the room (or shorten);

2. Move around the room and trade one thing with each person; and

3. Have each student take a turn being in the spotlight chair as classmates share the facts about the student.

Easing into Writing

Just as students need to be introduced in the classroom, there are writing activities to ease them into writing and sharing their

---

Figure 2.3
STUDENT SPOTLIGHTING FORM

Interesting and unusual things about me
(facts about me):

1. I have a lot of friends.
2. I am good at biking.
3. I play sports.
4. I have special Talents.
5. I am a good designer.
6. I am good at games.
7. I can Teach dogs Tricks.
8. I am a good Thinker.
9. I am a good reader.
10. I am good at art.
11. I am good at math.
12. I have moved Three Times in my life.
13. I like cats The most.
14. I like school.
15. I like To play.

—4Th grade

---

work. Add a few of these activities to your classroom routine, and students will begin to feel that the classroom is a safe and nurturing one for beginning writers.

Playing Classical Music During Writing

Teachers have been playing classical music during writing for a long time. Recently this practice has received a great deal of support from brain-based learning research, which says that classical music helps learners think well. Eric Jensen (1996) writes in *Brain-Based Learning*:

> Use music in your learning situations. Since each type of music can elicit a different type of psycho-physiological state, use a variety. When your learners arrive, you may want to play music that creates a state of anticipation or excitement (grand movie themes, upbeat classical). For storytelling, use music that has built-in peaks and valleys and engages fantasy and emotion (classical or romantic). For background you may want to use low volume Baroque. (p. 221)

I observed how music seems to work while visiting a friend and her new baby. During our visit, my friend put her baby into my arms and the baby immediately began to cry. The mother turned on the *Pachelbel Canon*. The baby stopped crying and began to look alertly from side to side. The baby didn't cry again while I was there. This was an amazing experience for me, for I believe that if music works on the most elemental level—for a newborn—then there must be something to it.

Setting a Timer

Use a digital kitchen timer that chimes at the end of a freewrite or any other timed activity. Tell students at the beginning of the activity that you are setting the timer, and then update them once or twice as to how many minutes they have left.

Putting Stamps on Freewrites

I have a set of stamps that I use to label students papers as they are freewriting. I use different stamps, such a butterfly for spring and a heart for Valentine's Day. I walk around the room and stamp papers as students write. I use the stamps instead of the date to keep

No matter what is wrong with you, a sausage biscuit will make you feel a whole lot better.

—*Lee Smith,*
"Lady Food," We Are What We Ate, *p. 203*

papers separated by day and also as a novelty. After students have been in my class for several months and I've gotten to know them, I use an "I love you" stamp. It is interesting to observe their responses. Some don't respond at all but just keep their heads down. Others keep their heads down, but you can see their cheeks broaden into smiles. Some look up and say aloud, "I love you, too, Ms. Worsham!" I think the response depends on how often they hear those words at home.

If you don't already tell students you love them, try it. You might be surprised at what those words do for classroom atmosphere and a student's willingness to write and learn.

Summary

Classroom atmosphere is extremely important in the teaching of writing, despite the age or ability level of your students. No one likes sharing with others without feeling safe, respected, and appreciated—even teachers! Many of the ideas in this chapter are suitable for immediate use. After establishing a safe, caring classroom environment, lead your students into the beginning stages of the writing process. Chapters 3 through 5 introduce a seven-step writing process and prewriting ideas that encourage and excite students about writing.

Suggestions for the Teacher

◆ Begin daily handshakes and standing ovations and watch what these activities do for your classroom.

◆ Let students make classroom banners with encouraging words—either sayings they create or find in books.

◆ Call a parent "for good reasons" and tell another teacher about this idea.

Sweet Potato Casserole

1 cup sugar

1/2 teaspoon salt

2 teaspoons all-purpose flour

1/2 teaspoon baking powder

3 cups cooked, mashed sweet potatoes

3 eggs, slightly beaten

1/2 cup milk

1/2 stick melted butter (4 tablespoons)

1 tablespoon vanilla

12 large marshmallows

◆ Preheat the oven to 350°. Mix together the dry ingredients. Add all of the other ingredients, except the marshmallows, to the dry mixture and combine thoroughly. Pour into a buttered baking dish.

◆ Bake the casserole until the potatoes are set, about 30 minutes. At the end of baking time, place the marshmallows on top of the casserole and return it to the oven just long enough to let the marshmallows brown.

Prewriting
and Drafting

3

WHEN MAKING HER SWEET POTATO CASSEROLE, MAMA PLACED MARSHMALLOWS carefully on top at the last minute, just in time for them to brown and form crisp golden tops. Then she took the dish out of the oven and set it on the table to cool. This was too much temptation for my sister Linda and me. At no time can I remember sitting down to eat the casserole with all the marshmallows in place. Always there were three or four little white syrupy craters where the stolen marshmallows had once been. I will never forget the taste and feel of those golden brown marshmallows with the soft melted centers. How delicious was the knowledge that, although we had stolen the marshmallows, no one was angry with us. We had been secretive and mischievous, and we had sneaked the best part early. Those warm, sweet marshmallows tasted like our mother's forgiveness. Prewriting, like the marshmallows on the top of my mother's sweet potato casserole, is the most fun and the best part.

Marjorie Frank calls the prewriting step "romancing." Romancing means having some of the best parts first. That step of prewriting is the time when writing is most exciting, when you are aware as a writer that creativity is sweet, and, at that point, it seems that everything you write is good.

What If They Just Won't?

Teachers sometimes ask me, "What if I have a student who just won't write?" Naturally, we need a sample of writing to be able to teach writing. But, how do you get that sample? Three parts of the expanded writing process are key to encouraging and coercing the most reluctant writers to begin to write.

The writing process, as described in most writing textbooks, is listed in five parts: (1) prewriting, (2) rough draft, (3) revision, (4) proofreading, and (5) final copy. I prefer, instead, a seven-step writing process that follows more closely the process used by successful writers:

1. Prewriting
2. Rough Draft
3. The Helping Circle
4. Revision
5. Proofreading
6. Final Copy
7. Publishing

Of these seven steps, the most effective parts for motivating students to write are prewriting, the helping circle, and publishing.

Prewriting is, of course, anything you do before you write. Prewriting includes topic selection, motivation, Marjorie Frank's romancing, and any of the myriad ways that writers get themselves in the mood to write. As Brenda Ueland (1987) writes, "The imagination needs moodling—long, inefficient, happy idling, dawdling and puttering" (p. 32). The prewriting we do with students should be fun and interesting. No one wants to write something that isn't interesting. As I was leaving an elementary class after teaching a writing assignment, a student ran to the door and said to me, "Your things are fun." If we are to motivate and encourage students, they need to feel that our writing assignments are fun. In this chapter are many

Do this: write every day . . . as fast and carelessly as you possibly can, without reading it again, anything you happened to have thought, seen, or felt the day before. . . . By taking it off on paper as fast as you can, you will not write what is dutiful and boring to you. . . . You will go straight to the point . . . if you write fast . . . you will touch only those things that interest you.

—Brenda Ueland,
If You Want to Write,
pp. 137–139

of my favorite prewriting activities. Some of these you may use as practice, and others you will follow through to publishing. You may try using several activities as practice and let students choose the writing they like best to finish. Other prewriting ideas are scattered throughout the book, especially in Chapters 4, 6, and 7.

Freewriting

Freewriting is especially good for loosening up and building fluency during the first stage of writing, the most personal and private stage. Freewriting means not thinking but just writing, keeping the pencil moving. Natalie Goldberg's (1991a) rules for what she calls writing practice are as follows: keep your hand moving; don't mark out words; don't fix spelling, punctuation, or grammar; do lose control; don't think; "[g]o for the jugular" (p. 8).

A good way for writing ideas to grow from freewriting is to get students to fill up a page (or one-half page for younger children) very rapidly without erasing or changing anything. They can then choose what they think is their best phrase or their best line and write that section at the top of a fresh sheet of paper. Then they ask the question, "What else can I say about that?" It's like looking for an inch of good stuff out of a mile of writing and then expanding on that inch.

I believe that students improve to a certain extent by regular personal freewriting, and therefore I suggest giving 10-minute freewrites every day at the beginning of the period. (For high school, you could require a minimum of 26 lines, margin to margin. For younger children, make it about a half a page, depending on the grade level.) Don't read these or respond to them. Just check them off and give students credit. Each freewrite is worth 20 points, to add up to a weekly grade of 100 points. Freewriting can also be used to help students generate ideas for a directed writing assignment. If you don't believe this idea works, try freewriting the next time you have a problem to solve or a decision to make.

Freewritings help you by providing no feedback at all. When I assign one, I invite the writer to let me read it. But also tell him to keep it if he prefers. I read it quickly and make no comments at all and I do not speak with him about it. The main thing is that a freewriting must never be evaluated in any way; in fact, there must be no discussion or comment at all.

—*Peter Elbow,*
Writing Without Teachers, *p. 4*

The Benefits of Freewriting

I believe in regular freewriting without teacher feedback— other than checking to see that it is done—and I'm not alone in this practice. Peter Elbow writes,

> The most effective way I know to improve your writing is to do freewriting exercises regularly. At least three times a week. They are sometimes called áutomatic writing,' babbling,' or Jabbering' exercises. The idea is simply to write for ten minutes (later on, perhaps fifteen or twenty). Don't stop for anything. Go quickly without rushing. Never stop to look back, to cross something out, to wonder how to spell something, or to wonder what word or thought to use, or to think about what you are doing. (p. 3)

When I was in graduate school, I did a research project in which I asked a class of 10th graders to write regularly for 10 minutes a day. I gave these students a pat on the back every now and then but no true feedback. At the end of three months, I studied the papers. I found that students not only increased in fluency—meaning that they wrote more words in the 10-minute period than they had at the beginning of the research period—but they also moved from short simple sentences, through a stage of long run-on sentences, to compound-complex sentences.

Not long after that research, I attended a workshop given by the writing researcher Mary Ellen Giacobbe. I took samples of student work to show her, and she told me that my students had moved from 1st to 3rd to 5th grade writing levels, simply by regular personal writing. If, however, I had marked their papers wrong as students moved into the run-on sentence stage, they would have gone back to the safer, simple sentences and would not have progressed to the more sophisticated sentence structures. They were, of course, still 10th grade writers writing on a 5th grade level, but we don't see that kind of progress often! Because students improve to a

That is why I hope you can keep up this continuity and sit for some time every day . . . before your typewriter, —if not writing, then just thoughtfully pulling your hair. If you skip for a day or two, it is hard to get started again.

—Brenda Ueland,
If You Want to Write,
p. 38

certain extent by regular personal writing, teachers need to make sure students write so that progress can happen.

Should I Give Journal Topics?

Teachers often ask if they should give students journal or freewrite topics. Usually, my answer is not to assign the topic. We want students to begin to see the writing possibilities in their own lives. If we give them ideas, they become dependent on our topics and don't look at the topics that their lives give them daily. Depending on their grade and writing level, you may offer students five tickets to use on "dry days." Keep topics in a shoe box—students turn in a ticket for the opportunity to draw a topic from the shoebox.

Beyond Freewriting: Drawing on Experience

Freewriting, or writing practice, is a routine warm-up for many writers. Sometimes it is just a warm-up exercise. Other times it can be used to jump-start the brainstorming process at the beginning of a writing assignment. Finally, prewriting activities may be more directed with a final, polished paper as the ultimate goal. As you and your students explore some of these techniques, don't be surprised if the students stumble upon a topic for writing about which they are very excited.

Experiencing with the Senses

Another good way to prewrite is to take students on an experience with their senses. E. Barrie Kavasch (1997) writes, "Through the lens of memory, I can look into the old oven and see Ma's biscuits rising, ghost biscuits from spirit batter and cloud dough tantalize my senses" (Avakian, p. 106). There are many ways to encourage students to experience their senses. Here are a few (pp. 42–43).

Just as we would never ask a child to multiply by six-digit numbers the first day of first grade, we shouldn't ask ourselves to begin page one of the great American novel the first day after we have realized our wish to write.

—Natalie Goldberg, Wild Mind: Living the Writer's Life, *p. 6*

Seeing

Show slides or pictures or a video with the sound turned off. Take students outside to look at everything.

Hearing

Play tapes of different sounds. Or, blindfold your students and take them outside and ask them to listen.

Smelling

Soak several cotton balls in different fragrances or smells, from perfume to onions, and put them in film canisters. Then let students smell the collection and write about what they smell.

Tasting

Show students the differences among sweet, sour, bitter, and other flavors by letting them taste different foods.

Feeling and Touching

Put items with different textures in a shoebox with a hole in the end. Let students put their hands in and feel each texture, one at a time. Be sure to include yucky things like the imitation eyeballs you can find in stores just before Halloween.

Feeling and Emotions

Point out the difference between feeling as touching and feeling as emotions. Have students write about a time when their feelings were hurt.

Place Writing

Identify familiar places in your town and write them on index cards, remembering to include the grocery store, the laundromat, a church or temple or mosque, the mall, a restaurant, a car wash, a beauty shop, a bank, and a gas station. Randomly hand out index cards to the students and ask them to write a thorough description of the place, using all five senses. Remind students to write what they see, hear, smell, taste, and touch in the place. After writing the descriptions, let students read the descriptions aloud. Place writing is a good activity for beginning the practice of reading aloud because the writing is in the short form of a paragraph. In addition, students can hear how vivid writing becomes when authors appeal to the senses.

Hazel's Story

In this age of student ridicule and the violence that often accompanies it, this is a good activity to help increase students' tolerance and sensitivity to the feelings of others. Drawing from your childhood, share your experience about a person who was picked on.

I tell students about Alice, who was in the 7th grade with me. Alice came from a poor family, and each morning when she came into the classroom, students would lean to the side to avoid being touched by her. If she happened to brush close to someone's desk, the student would say, "Ooh!" and touch someone nearby, saying, "You've got Alice's cooties!" I explain to students that I didn't make fun of her, but I didn't take up for her; I confess how I feel about that today.

After introducing this subject by sharing with students your own story, read aloud, "Hazel's Story," in Figure 3.1 (p. 44). After you read the story, ask students to write about someone they remember who often got picked on. Ask students to change the names of the students in the story because many of your students probably grew up together.

One time when my students were working on this activity, a student came up to my desk and said, "Ms. Worsham, I was the one everybody always picked on. They still do." My response was to ask him to write about how that makes him feel.

What people don't realize is that writing is physical. It doesn't have to do with thought alone. It has to do with sight, smell, taste, feeling, with everything being alive and activated.

—Natalie Goldberg,
Writing Down the Bones,
p. 50

Figure 3.1
HAZEL'S STORY

Her name was Hazel, and all my classmates hated her. Actually, they didn't really hate her, but they acted like it. Every day at recess, she stood by herself against a tree. No one would play with her. When we played kickball, she would stand and watch, and no one would ever ask her to play. One day someone kicked the ball out of bounds, and it rolled over to Hazel's tree. She bent down and picked it up and threw it back, and then no one would play with the ball anymore. If that had happened to me, I wouldn't be able to stop crying, but Hazel never cried.

At lunchtime, she sat at a table all by herself. She had long black hair that she pulled back into a ponytail with a little ribbon. As she sat at the table by herself eating, she took little tiny bites and ate slowly and daintily.

One day during geography Hazel went to the teacher's desk and asked to go to the bathroom. The teacher, Mrs. Meriwether, made her write her name on the board. That meant she would have to stay after school for going to the bathroom during class.

But then Hazel didn't come back for a long time. We had already finished Bolivia and were about to start long division when Mrs. Meriwether noticed that Hazel was still gone. Then she pointed at me. "Mary Harkness," she said, "Go to the girls' bathroom and check on Hazel." Everybody turned and looked at me, and I could feel my face turning red.

(continued)

Figure 3.1
(continued)

As I Turned The corner To go in The bathroom, I could hear Hazel being sick. When I got There, she was down on her knees in one of The stalls Throwing up. I stood There for a little while, and Then I said, "Mrs. Meriwether said for me To come check."

Hazel came out and went To The sink and splashed water on her face and wiped her face with a paper Towel. Then she looked at me. Her eyes were black and sparkly, and I noticed That she had long, curly eyelashes. "Thank you for coming," she said.

"Is There anyThing I can do?" I asked her. "Are you going To be okay?"

"Yes," she said. Then she looked at my dress where I had pinned a little leather dog pin That matched my dress. It had a Thin red ribbon Tied around Its neck. "I have a dog," she said. "I like your pin."

"Thank you," I said. And Then It seemed like my hands started moving without me. They reached up and Took off The dog pin and gave It To her. "Here," I said. "You can have It."

She started To say no, and Then she reached out and Took It. She held It in her hand, looking down.

Then, when she looked up, I saw That she was crying. Hazel, who never cried, was crying.

And Then she smiled at me. And I smiled back. And I felt like The happiest person in The world.

—Mary Harkness, 7Th grade

After writing his story, he volunteered to read it aloud. As he read, the class was completely silent. When he finished, a female student stood and addressed the class. "You see how we make people feel?" she asked. "Everybody's got feelings." It was a wonderful, teachable moment that sometimes happens in a classroom—one that can't be tested academically but is immensely important in other ways. Beginning that day, those students began to treat that young man with greater respect.

Graveyard Story

Newspaper articles are a wonderful resource for finding writing ideas. An article I found in a newspaper is one of my favorite prewriting activities. In this article, a California firm announces the availability of a talking gravestone. Instead of an engraved inscription, the company advertises a gravestone equipped to play the deceased's (prerecorded) message for 40 years. Friends, family, and strangers can walk by the grave, push a button, and hear the voice of the deceased.

For the writing activity, have students plan and write the script for the tape they would leave behind. After you have done this

---

Figure 3.2
GRAVEYARD STORY

To all of you who are ouT There missing me, I wanT To say I miss you Too, especially Timmy my frog and my dog Sam. Sam, don'T go in The neighbor's yards To do your business. John, you have To do all my chores now Too, so do Them good. Janice, sTay ouT of my sTuff, or I'll come back To haunT you. Mama, I'm sorry for all The Times I was bad and didn'T clean up my room. I love you, Jack

—3rd grade

Figure 3.3
Mason's Graveyard Story

I would want to say hey to all of my family, and I love them. And I would want to say something to all of my children if I have any. Don't let nobody tell you anything wrong, and don't get involved with any gangs because some of them don't care about you. Find a job that will provide for your family, and stay in touch with each other. I'll be watching out for y'all from up in Heaven, and I love y'all.

—Mason, 9th grade

---

activity several times, you may read samples from former students to help get the class started. Figures 3.2 and 3.3 are two of my favorites.

Church Story

Read aloud to students the story called "Salvation," about Langston Hughes when he was a teenager. It's about his experience of being in church and not being saved when everyone else was "seeing Jesus come to them" (Hughes, 1940, pp. 18–21). After reading this story, ask students to write a church (or synagogue or mosque) story. Through this activity, I have heard baptism stories, Easter speech stories, and Bible school stories. One of my favorite church stories is by Michael Fraley, a 10th grader (see Figure 3.4, p. 48). You may want to read Michael's story aloud as a sample.

The church story idea was first published in "Five Good Writing Ideas" (Worsham, 2000). Another favorite story is by Gladys Mitchell (see Figure 3.5, p. 49). Figure 3.6 (p. 50) is a sample temple story, and Figure 3.7 (p. 51) is a sample mosque story.

Figure 3.4
SAVED FROM SIN

When I was little, I used To go To Sunday School on Sundays; at least, They Thought That was where I was gone. I used To get a quarter To put in church. But The quarter never got There. Every Sunday, my friend Bernard and I used To go To The church and go down in The basement and crawl out of The window and go To The store and buy candy.

When we left The store, we used To go on The other side of The railroad Track and fish unTil one o'clock. We didn't even go To church on Easter although we had new suits, and I even had an Easter speech. When it was Time for me To say my speech, I Told my cousin To say I was in The bathroom sick. But I was really on The other side of The Track fishing.

One Sunday while we were skipping Sunday School, we went down The stream farTher Than we had ever been. We found an old boaT and got in. When we got in The middle, it starTed To sink. NeiTher of us could swim, buT somehow we made it To land. We ran all The way back To church and climbed back in The window and went upsTairs. When we got up There, They asked us why were we wet. I Told Them we had been bapTized and saved.

—Michael Fraley, 10th grade

Source: Published in the 1985 *Rain Dance Review* by Baldwin High School. Used with permission.

Figure 3.5
JOINING CHURCH

I remember when I first joined church. It was one of our spring revivals. My mother made Janey and me sit on The front bench of The church.

After The Reverend got Through preaching, he came down out of The pulpit and said, Doors of The church open. Our mother poked us and made us go sit in The chairs in The front.

The preacher came over and asked us our names and asked us how long we wanted To be members of The church. We just sat There, until Mama leaned over and whispered, Tell him, Until I die.

After That we went To church in white sheets with a Towel Tied around our heads. The deacon was singing Take Me To The Water. The next Thing I knew, The preacher ducked me under, and The water went up my nose.

Then The mother of The church Told us To go sit on a special bench, and Janey and I felt special That whole night.

—Gladys Mitchell, 5Th grade

Source: Published in the 1985 *Rain Dance Review* by Baldwin High School. Used with permission.

Students who do not have experiences and stories they wish to share from religious backgrounds may use other group experiences and stories—from 4-H, Boy or Girl Scouts, Boys' and Girls' Clubs, or sports teams.

Crime Digest

If you can find a small-town newspaper close to you, subscribe immediately! In its pages are many writing activities. My town,

Figure 3.6
TEMPLE STORY

I went To Temple with my Mommy and Daddy and Zedah Freda last night. It was Rosh Hashanah. Gramma came on The bus with her friends from The Robinson Jewish Home where she lives. We went To Temple BeTh Israel. I wore my new dress. That is because Rosh Hashanah is The new year. I saw my Third grade SabbaTh School Teacher from last year. She is Ms. Goldman and she was with her boyfriend. He is very good-looking. We read from The book That Mr. Heiman, The usher, gave us when we came in. The rabbi came To our house for dinner last monTh for my daddy's birThday. My daddy helped To build The Temple. I don'T Know exactly whaT he did buT iT is beauTiful. IT has sTained glass windows and a special place for The Torah. I will read from The Torah on my baT miTzvah when I am ThirTeen. AfTer The service we had cookies. I had Three buT Then we had To go home.

—BeThany Cohen, 4Th grade

Milledgeville, has a newspaper called the *Union-Recorder*. Like many small-town newspapers, this paper contains a regular section that reports criminal activity in our town. These reports are about things that happen to real people, and the way they are written is often amusing.

I give these reports to students and ask them to imagine the people behind the samples and to write a story about them. Samples are in Figure 3.8 (p. 52). Try to find small-town newspapers and humorous samples in your own locale. If you live in a very small

---

Figure 3.7
MOSQUE STORY

Friday is a special day, we always gather up to pray. Since our school is right across from the Mosque, we all walk there with our Teachers. They tell us to sit down and listen to a speech. After prayer we're supposed to go back to school with our Teachers. Well I sneak out and play on the side of the Mosque.

One day it was snowing and I did the same thing I always do. My friends and I were Throwing snow balls at each other. Two of my friends left and one stayed with me. We made fun of a man and Threw snowballs at his car. Then we played with the snow some more. The principal saw us and we got in Trouble. I havn't done That since.

—Sarah Swan, age 9

---

town, be careful about using samples that may involve relatives of your students. You may want to subscribe to a newspaper from a town other than your own. You may also try carefully selecting weird happenings from those "news" magazines you find at the grocery store check-out line!

Alexander

Judith Viorst's (1987) wonderful little book entitled *Alexander and the Terrible, Horrible, No Good, Very Bad Day* is a good resource for prewriting. Read this book to students and then ask them to write about *their* very bad day. Figure 3.9 (p. 53) shows some samples of this activity.

Figure 3.8
CRIME DIGEST SAMPLES

I have gathered the following excerpts from a local paper. Local papers offer wonderful story starters.

Someone poured syrup on the hood of a 1995 Nissan Altima on Wednesday or Thursday in the 1600 block of Valley Road. (June 23–25, 2001, page 3A)

A screen door was stolen from a house Wednesday in the 400 block of Gumm Cemetery Road. (June 23–25, 2001, page 3A)

A business sign at Buddy's Recycling in the 500 block of North Wayne Street was stolen Thursday or Friday. (Tuesday, June 26, 2001, page 3A)

A screen door believed stolen from a house in the 400 block of Gumm Cemetery road last week was found Thursday. The door was being repaired by a friend while the owner was out of town. (Tuesday, June 26, 2001, page 3A)

A waiter displeased with getting too small a tip Thursday night got hit in the throat after confronting the frugal customer. It happened at a restaurant in the 2400 block of North Columbia Street when the waiter, cleaning off the table, noticed his customer had left him 10 pennies as a tip. Angry, the waiter followed the man out into the parking lot and threw the pennies at him, prompting the fracas. The suspect took off and was not found by police.

Someone broke a car window in the 1400 block of south Elbert Street sometime Thursday or Friday and took a Bible with a leather cover.

Someone shattered a window in a home in the 400 block of West Charlton Street on Wednesday, entered the home, and ate a large portion of leftovers from the refrigerator. The suspect left the plate and part of the meal on the side porch.

A 34-year-old woman reported Friday that someone stole her stuffed mannequin from her backyard. The mannequin is made of cloth, with glass eyes, a brown tweed coat, brown boots, cream-colored pants, and wears a hat. His name is "Joe," the woman reported.

Source: Used and adapted by permission of the *Union-Recorder.* Copyright 1981–2001.

Scars

A teacher at a workshop shared this idea with me: Everywhere on our body that we have a scar, including in our hearts, we have a story. The next step is to translate the idea into drawing and writing. For example, refer to the drawing in Figure 3.10 (p. 54) and draw a

Figure 3.9
VERY BAD DAYS

One morning I got up late couldn't take a bath because of the hot water. I couldn't find anything to wear there was no more cereal and I missed the bus and got to school at 9:00 a.m. Then I got in trouble for coming to school and had to sit in the sun when it was time to play.

—3rd grade

One morning I woke up and missed the bus because I forgot to iron my clothes. Then when I got to school I forgot all my homework and lost 2 points. Then when I got on the bus, I forgot the rule boys on one side and girls on the other, and everybody started calling me a boy. When I got home, I was locked out of the house. Then when I went to play with my friends I had to get a perm. Then that night I went home and got sick from eating too much. I had a terrible, horrible, no good, very bad day.

—5th grade

One day I went to school with a very bad hair day. My hair was sticking out. I put my coat on my head and the teacher said take my coat off and I did not. She put my name on the board. That was my very bad day.

—6th grade

picture of yourself on the chalkboard. Next, draw an arrow to the places where you have scars and share a story or two about the scars with your students. Then, ask students to draw themselves and to indicate their scars by drawing arrows. After that, the students go a step further and write a story about one of their scars.

In response to this activity, one 3rd grader wrote: "The way I got my scars was on a summer day I was jumping on a trampoline and then I fell through the springs and I got 5 scars. And my brother was laughing." Figures 3.11 and 3.12 (p. 55) are other samples of writing about scars. Note that one student created a legend for the drawing.

Writing from Reading

Use modeling to illustrate how students can glean writing ideas from reading. Begin to read aloud a short story with your students. As soon as something you read makes you think of something you can write, stop reading and tell students about your idea. Next, ask

Figure 3.10
SCARS DRAWING

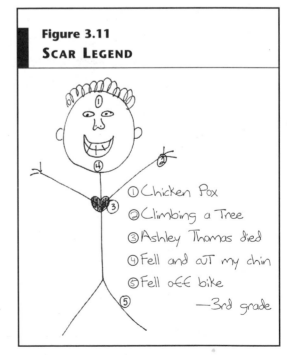

Figure 3.11
SCAR LEGEND

Figure 3.12
SCAR STORY

One my are I got burnt by The iron and below my Knee
I fell on skates and on The side of my eye I hit it on The
desk and on my nose I hit it on The holer for The Toliet
Tissue Thing.

—4Th grade

---

them to work in groups to do the same thing. Give students books—perhaps anthologies of short stories—and let them read aloud and share ideas as they come. The groups can make a list of possible writing topics.

Writing in a Place

If you can manage this with the grade level you teach, give this assignment as homework. Ask students to go to a specific place in town and just sit and write about what they see. Great places include grocery stores, laundromats, churches, and the downtown area. They should write everything they see, hear, smell, taste, and touch. Tell them to write physical descriptions of people and to record conversations they overhear. If the out-of-school assignment is too difficult in your setting, ask them to observe and write within the school—in the gymnasium, the cafeteria, the front office, the auditorium, or another classroom.

A Writer's Notebook

A good practice is to have students keep the work they do in a classroom notebook, folder, or portfolio. Let them create their own cover and make the notebook *theirs*. Not only will you have something to show parents and school board members, but also students

A writer who is following a plan and keeping within it suddenly goes off in a new, unexpected direction. The writer's mind seems almost to have developed a life and will of its own, and he or she looks with amazement on what has been written.

—James E. Miller, Jr., and Stephen N. Judy, Writing in Reality, *p. 21*

themselves can look through their notebooks and see improvement throughout the course or year. Often their own improvement is amazing to students: "I can't believe I wrote that much!" or "Look how much better I can write now!"

Rough Draft

After the prewriting step comes the rough draft, that time when students actually work on writing the paper for the first time. Like those of successful writers, these first drafts can be messy and full of mistakes and may also be called "discovery drafts" or "the sloppy copy."

Many writers have much to say about this stage of writing. Eve Shelnutt (1989) writes, "In a first draft, write everything down. . . . let yourself go. Don't censor yourself" (p. 209). Bernard Malamud states in *The Writers' Chapbook,* "The first draft of a book is the most uncertain—where you need guts, the ability to accept the imperfect until it is better" (Plimpton, 1989, p. 130). Henry Miller, in the *Writers at Work* series, says, "I never do any correcting or revising while in the process of writing. Let's say I write a thing out any old way, and then, after it's cooled off . . . I see it with a fresh eye" (Plimpton, 1963, p. 170). Writers see this stage of writing as a time for uncovering the treasures in their subconscious, a process which begins, of course, with prewriting and continues in the rough draft stage.

The rough draft stage allows us to be totally absorbed. Look at the faces of students as they write to see that expression we all get, regardless of our age, when we are totally absorbed in the wonderful world of our imaginations. During the rough draft stage, writers of all ages need to be allowed time to let their ideas develop; time to be natural writers.

While using the writing process, you and your students will find that sometimes the lines between the steps become blurred. In teaching the specific steps, we prepare students to become better writers, but writers of all ages and at all levels often double back, maybe stopping a rough draft to prewrite again or perhaps turning

The unconscious must flow freely and richly bringing at demand all the treasures of memory, all the emotions, incidents, scenes, intimations of character and relationship which it has stored away in its depths.

—Dorothea Brande,
Becoming a Writer, *p. 45*

a prewrite into a rough draft. For the purposes of teaching writing, each step is distinct; in reality, though, these steps of creativity cannot be so clearly defined.

In my classroom, I sometimes offer many prewriting activities and then allow students to choose their favorite to turn into a rough draft. Other times I select a favorite prewriting activity that almost always produces good writing from students, and I lead the whole class through the process together, starting with a specific prewriting assignment and following through to the end. In this chapter, the scars activity is one of these favorites that I often ask students to follow through the entire process, rather than just using it for practice. In Chapter 4 you'll find two other prewriting assignments that are reliable enough to be "whole process" papers—the childhood memory story (p. 77) and the house story (p. 81).

In a year's worth of writing with your students, I suggest you do several prewriting activities during every two-week period and have students follow through one activity to a final draft about every third week. The schedule depends on the grade and ability levels of your students, as well as how you feel about the writing your students perform. In addition, *any* prewriting assignment, including freewriting, can be a final paper for a grade or for publishing if it is an idea that works with your students, piques their imaginations, and produces a paper that they are excited about and can be proud of.

Remember that the best way we can *teach* writing is to *model* writing. *Show* the students your sloppy copy. Let them see *you* with that wonderful look of concentration on *your* face!

Summary

Prewriting is time to play with our ideas, to motivate, lead, inspire, and excite. We need to model by writing for our students, letting them see that we believe that writing is a fun and important thing to do. Prewriting leads naturally into the next stage, during which each child completes a rough or discovery draft.

When I look around at people writing, I can tell just by their physical posture if they have broken through or not. If they did, their teeth are rattling around in their mouth, no longer tight in their gums; their hearts might be pounding or aching. They are breathing deeply. Their handwriting is looser, more generous, and their bodies are relaxed enough to run for miles.

—Natalie Goldberg,
Writing Down the Bones,
p. 50

Usually at the step of a complete rough draft, the writer, whether famous or not, feels exhilaration and wants to share with others. Hart Crane is described as emerging after a long session of writing and "appearing in the doorway, his eyes burning, his face red, his hair standing on end, and saying, 'Read that. Isn't that the greatest poem ever written!' " (Rugg, 1963, p. 16). This is the way we feel after working hard on a rough draft. At that point, we are ready and eager to share our writing with others. The sharing time, or helping circle, leads us to Chapter 4.

Suggestions for the Teacher

◆ Freewrite with your students, sitting near them as they write. After 10 minutes, share with them what you have written. Share with them your surprises, those places where you wrote something you didn't know you were going to write.

◆ Let students talk in groups about possible topics they might like to write about from their lives. Move from group to group, listening and sharing topics of your own. This practice helps students start to notice the writing ideas in their everyday lives and makes writing itself a topic for discussion.

◆ Occasionally play different kinds of music during writing time and watch your students get lost in their own imaginations.

Friendship Bread

To "feed" the starter:

1 cup starter from a friend

2 cups sugar

2 cups all-purpose flour

2 cups milk

To make the bread:

1 cup starter

2/3 cup oil

1 cup sugar

3 eggs, beaten until blended

1 teaspoon vanilla

1 large box instant vanilla pudding mix

2 cups all-purpose flour

1/2 teaspoon baking soda

1 1/4 teaspoons baking powder

2 teaspoons cinnamon

1/2 teaspoon salt

1/2 to 1 cup chopped nuts

For the Starter

◆ Day 1: The day you receive the starter, leave it in an open container on the kitchen counter. (If you *have* to begin this by yourself, mix together 1 cup sugar, 1 cup all-purpose flour, and 1 cup milk and follow the directions from here. This really *isn't* the way to do it, however, and your recipe, while good, will get much better as the starter is passed from friend to friend.)

◆ Days 2, 3, and 4: Stir the starter with a wooden spoon once. Store uncovered on the counter.

◆ Day 5: Add 1 cup sugar, 1 cup flour, and 1 cup milk.

◆ Days 6, 7, 8, and 9: Stir the starter with a wooden spoon *once.* Store uncovered on the counter.

◆ Day 10: Add 1 cup sugar, 1 cup flour, and 1 cup milk. The starter is now ready to be made into bread. Measure the starter into separate cups and put into containers to give to friends, or make bread. You can divide the three cups any way you wish. You could bake one loaf of bread, keep one starter, and give away one starter or one loaf of bread.

For the Bread

◆ Preheat the oven to 325°. Mixing by hand with a wooden spoon (do *not* use an electric mixer), combine the starter, oil, sugar, eggs, vanilla, and pudding mix. In a separate bowl, sift together the flour, baking soda, baking powder, cinnamon, and salt. Then fold the flour mixture into the starter mixture and fold in the nuts.

◆ Pour the batter into a buttered bundt pan or loaf pans. Sprinkle the top of the loaf with sugar. Bake for 60 to 70 minutes or until done. Do not undercook. The bread is done when it bounces back from being touched in the center or when a cake tester comes out clean. If the batter clings to the tester, the bread should be baked longer.

Learning to Use
the Helping Circle

4

FRIENDSHIP BREAD IS NOT A RECIPE THAT YOU SHOULD START BY YOURSELF AND END by yourself. The bread and the starter have to be shared, like writing, if it's to achieve its purpose of nourishing. Mama and I figured out that it *is* possible to begin your own starter, but that isn't the right way to make Friendship bread. You are supposed to get your starter from a friend, and you are supposed to share your starter (and the bread, of course) with another friend.

Mama often had two little loaves of Friendship bread, side-by-side on the table, ready to deliver to friends. On another table would be a bowl containing starter, waiting its turn. Friendship bread, like writing, gets better when it is given time to develop, and when it is shared with friends. After writers finish their rough drafts, they are not ready to begin revising until they have shared their work with others, usually a peer group, and received response.

The Helping Circle

The helping circle, the step in the writing process that follows the rough draft, is an amazing thing. This step is something akin to a miracle in the way it helps students with writing. Using the methods of practicing writers, the helping circle teaches beginning writers to help one another with their writing.

At Yaddo everything revolves around food. The food here is plentiful and exquisite (last night, an amazing sea bass . . .) though the real blessing is the way the food provides each day's productively self-indulgent structure. . . . For the rest of my life, whenever I taste sea bass, I'll be back here.

—Mark Winegardner,
We Are What We Ate, p. 15

61

For years teachers have followed a model of teaching writing that dictated that students write individually for their teacher's eyes only. The teacher, the classroom expert, makes the assignments. The students write the assignments and give them to the teacher. The teacher spends many hours grading these papers, and then returns them to the students. What actually happens, however, when the students get the papers back? Do the many hours the teacher spent working with papers actually balance with the amount of learning that takes place when the papers are returned to the students? Is this model really working to make our students better writers? Do the students even review and retain the feedback given by teachers?

In a more successful model, the teacher is one member of the group, not the resident expert. When shown how to work in this model, the students learn how to help one another with their writing, and everyone becomes an expert.

The idea of the helping circle originated with Ken Macrorie (1976):

> Almost every good writer has learned to write in circles. First, she writes for herself and then reads aloud her writing and listens. It sounds different, as if it had made a circle and become someone else's writing. She can judge it better.

> Second, she reads it to a friend or member of the family. Now it sounds different from the way it did when she read it to herself. She begins to sense how the writing may come across to another person who didn't share the experiences and feelings she wrote about. The listener doesn't have to say anything, but simply be there—and the writing becomes an object apart from the writer. She's objective about it. (p. 63)

The helping circle, as I use it, is a group of people working together to accomplish a task: making each paper in the circle a better paper. Out of this circle grows a deeper knowledge—not about what good writing is to the teacher, but about what good writing is, period.

Students, like published authors, share their writing with their peers, the people whose opinions matter most to them. Regardless of age or ability level, all students can be taught to help one another with their writing. Student writers can, in fact, become helpers as proficient as their teachers. "Writing is not just writing," Natalie Goldberg (1991a) reminds us (p. 80). "It is also having a relationship with other writers."

How the Helping Circle Looks

The helping circle isn't really a circle. It is instead a group of students whose desks are pushed into a cluster in the center of the room so that their heads are close together. As opposed to a circle, which produces a large intimidating space in the middle of the formation, this arrangement is more intimate.

The Helping Circle Procedure

Here is a quick overview of the way the helping circle works best.

1. One person reads his rough draft while everyone else makes notes on either three or six things to listen for (e.g., what the listener likes, where the author can add more, questions from the listener, honesty, voice, and mind pictures).

2. The listeners use their notes to respond orally to the reader's rough draft.

3. The reader records the comments on his rough draft.

4. The reader reads back the notes to the listeners.

5. The next member of the helping circle reads her rough draft.

What to Listen for

Whether listeners work on a list of three things or six things depends on their sophistication. Regardless of the age or ability level, it is best to use only the first three on the list when just beginning to

The two persons she was, gifted cook and lover of ideas, found expression in Mama's kitchen. We never simply ate her cooking; we feasted on her love for polemics. Family meals were, for us, intellectual gatherings.

—Marie Smyth,
"Hedge Nutrition, Hunger, and Irish Identity," Through the Kitchen Window, *p. 100*

use the helping circle (what the listener likes, where the author can add more, and questions from the listener).

Places the Listener Likes

Much of learning to write is figuring things out for ourselves. As teachers, our job is to create conditions such that students can figure out for themselves how to write. At the helping circle we aren't working on grammar, usage, or mechanics. That comes later with proofreading. The helping circle prepares students for revision, or re-vision—seeing again. Writers of all ages don't realize where they have succeeded until their listeners tell them, and we learn much more from being told where we have succeeded than where we have failed. When students read at the helping circle, they are often surprised at the responses they receive, the laughter at a certain part, or that "Ah!" sound, coming from their listeners. As writers, we learn from these responses how to strengthen our writing. Even kindergarteners are good at raising their hands and telling the author which parts of a story they like.

Where the Author Can Add More

Writing is like an iceberg. What the author puts on paper is only the part above the water; what's underneath the water is still in the writer's mind. When the author reads her own work, she sees the total picture, not just the part on the paper. The members of the helping circle can help the author see which parts are still in her mind and not on the paper. Peer response fills in specific details that flesh out mental images in writing. From *The House of Fiction*, an excellent book on writing compiled by Caroline Gordon and Allen Tate (1960), we find,

An amateur writer usually puts only half of his story on paper. . . . He reads the story over and sees, not the story he has written but the story he had hoped to write and had partially conceived. To distinguish between the actual story and the imagined story one

---

You will never be working from grim, dry willpower but from generosity and the fascinating search for truth. Your motto: Be Bold, be Free, be Truthful. The truthfulness will save it from flamboyance, from pretentiousness.

—Brenda Ueland,
If You Want to Write, p. X

must, as it were, follow the painter's practice of stepping back from
the easel to survey the work with narrowed, coldly critical, and self-
excluding eyes. (p. 456)

Questions We Still Have

The questions posed by listeners in the helping circle indicate
what information the writer has left out. Listeners often ask "How
old were you?" and "Were you scared?" Young children are especially good at thinking of questions. Sometimes, the questions the
listeners ask overlap with suggestions of where the author can add
more to the story. It seems to help students, however, to be told to
listen for both. The helping circle assists student writers in seeing the
whole story with a more objective viewpoint.

Honesty

Honesty in writing doesn't mean confessional writing. It means
writing only what you really believe to be true—no fake emotions.
An activity to help students understand honesty in writing is to ask
them to write something private on a piece of paper, something
that nobody else knows. Then they should read it to themselves and
see how it sounds. They may then tear it up and throw it away. The
teacher can carry around the trash can and let everyone throw away
their honest writing. Also, the teacher can collect sections of good,
honest writing from literature to read aloud to students as examples.
She can also share examples of her own honest writing with them.

Many established authors have written about honesty in writing. Ken Macrorie (1976) writes,

> All good writers speak in honest voices and tell the truth. . . . This is
> the first requirement for good writing: truth; not *The* truth (who-
> ever knows surely what that is?), but some kind of truth—a connec-
> tion between the things written about, the words used in the writ-
> ing, and the author's experience in a world she knows well—
> whether in fact or dream or imagination (p. 5).

The idea of writing honestly is difficult to explain to students and much easier to show by actual helping circle examples. Honest writing is closely connected to growth and development. Young children, for example, don't really know how to write in dishonest ways. As children grow, however, and they reach middle and high school, they begin to ask: "Who am I?" "What do I think?" "What do I feel?" "What is acceptable to my peers?" You can't belabor the point of honest writing. You just have to listen for examples of honest writing in the helping circle and point them out to students. In almost all cases, as long as students write what they know and have experienced, their writing will be honest.

If, for example, a student who has never experienced a major loss in her family tries to write about the death of a friend or family member, the writing is apt to be filled with sentimentality. Laurence Perrine (1970) writes,

> Sentimentality is not the same as genuine emotions. Sentimentality is contrived or excessive or faked emotion. A story contains genuine emotion when it treats life faithfully and perceptively. The sentimentalized story oversimplifies and sweetens life to get its feeling. It exaggerates, manipulates, and prettifies. It mixes tears with sugar. (p. 275)

Just encourage students to write from their own experience and then listen for honest examples as they read their works aloud. Before you know it, your students will be using the phrase, "That was so honest," at the helping circle, for their classmates will show them what honest writing is, and they will understand.

Voice

Writing honestly almost guarantees that students write in their natural voice. Tell students that their writing should *sound* like them, like the voice inside their head. Say, "Write like you!" Voice in writing is the same as *tone of voice* in speaking. Anne Lamott

As a child, he spoke and wrote honestly most of the time, but when he reaches fifteen, honesty and truth come harder. The pressures on his ego are greater. He reaches for impressing language; often it is pretentious and phony.

—Ken Macrorie,
Telling Writing, *p. 6*

(1995) reminds us, "The truth of your experience can only come through in your own voice. If it is wrapped in someone else's voice, we readers will feel suspicious, as if you are dressed up in someone else's clothes" (p. 199).

An activity that helps students understand voice is to have them write something in the most honest voice they can use without putting their names on their paper. Then the teacher reads selections aloud, and the class tries to guess who wrote it. Another idea is to give students selections of writing by established authors who have distinctive styles—Ernest Hemingway, William Faulkner, Mark Twain, Zora Neale Hurston—and let them attempt to imitate the style of these writers.

One of my favorite sources of student activities for teaching voice is the book *Inside Out: Developmental Strategies for Teaching Writing* by Dan Kirby and Tom Liner (1981). Among many other voice ideas, one is "Mad Talking, Soft Talking, Fast Talking" (p. 142), in which students do three 10-minute freewrites. In the first one, students freewrite about things that make them angry. In the second freewrite, they comfort someone; and in the third, they persuade someone. They then go back and study the differences they see in the three freewrites, including such things as word choice and sentence length. This activity helps students to learn to *hear* their own voices in writing.

Mind Pictures

Mind pictures are the images you see in your mind as you read; they are the images you cause the listener to see through your writing. Mind pictures are brought on by appealing to all of the senses, having students write what they see, hear, smell, taste, and touch. For example, ask students, "When you think about a bicycle, what do you see in your mind?" Expect students to be puzzled or hesitant. Then say to them, "Now, suppose I say 'a rusty little pink bicycle with a banana seat.' " Students will then *see* the picture in their minds, and they'll be able to see what mind pictures do.

An activity that teaches mind pictures is to read aloud this selection from *To Kill a Mockingbird,* by Harper Lee (1960):

Maycomb was an old town, but it was a tired old town when I first knew it. In rainy weather the streets turned to red slop; grass grew on the sidewalks, the courthouse sagged in the square. Somehow, it was hotter then: a black dog suffered on a summer's day; bony mules hitched to Hoover carts flicked flies in the sweltering shade of the live oaks on the square. Men's stiff collars wilted by nine in the morning. Ladies bathed before noon, after their three o'clock naps, and by nightfall were like soft teacakes with frostings of sweat and sweet talcum. (p. 11)

Ask students which words help them see the image. Using the passage as a sample, have students write a paragraph about their own town or a particular place in town; remind them to appeal to the senses to create mind pictures. Read the descriptions aloud in small groups and have the other members of the group identify the words that best "show" the picture.

Another mind picture activity is to distribute magazines, student literary magazines, or newspapers, and ask students to find five good mind pictures. Have students read aloud the mind pictures in small groups or with the whole class to bring the idea alive.

A particularly wonderful mind picture of sound can be found in the beginning of "Knoxville: Summer, 1915" from James Agee's *A Death in the Family* (1938). It is a description of the sounds a water hose makes when ranging from a thin spray to short bursts and the sounds of the locusts and crickets in the evening.

Out of any one hose, the almost dead silence of the release, and the short still arch of the separate big drops, silent as a held breath, and the only noise the flattering noise on leaves and the slapped grass at the fall of each big drop. . . . The noise of each locust is pitched in some classic locust range out of which none of them varies more than two full tones. (pp. 4–5)

Students new to the helping circle need extra instruction and practice with the six things to listen for. The helping circle itself, however, teaches all six items better than any separate exercise. At the helping circle, students hear many samples of good writing from their classmates. As they sit and listen, light bulbs click on in their heads. As teacher, present with them in the circle, you can watch it happen. They whisper to each other, "I could do that!" and "That happened to me!" They even say, "Oh, now I get it!" And those are words teachers love to hear!

Teaching the Helping Circle

Imagine that your students have just finished a rough draft, and it is time to teach the helping circle for the first time. Ask students to put their rough drafts on their desks. If this is new to you, feel free to tell students that you are all just trying this method together to see how it works.

Next, ask students to arrange desks into a whole-class cluster in the center of the room. Help them the first time or two by saying "Howard, pull your desk up here; Susie, you scoot in right here; Lester, pull your desk in close behind Ron." After students have learned how a helping circle *looks*, you will be able to say, "Make a helping circle, One-Two-Three-Four-Five!" and students will have desks arranged in the helping circle formation in about a minute. At the end of the period, students will be able to disband the helping circle in a similar amount of time.

Join the circle and give each student a piece of paper with either three or six things they should listen for (Figures 4.1 and 4.2, p. 70). If the class is just beginning to use the helping circle, just ask for the first three things. Explain that each person will read a draft while the others listen and take notes, and that you will model the process with the first reader.

As the first student reads a rough draft, ask the other students to observe as you model taking notes. As you listen to the student's rough draft being read aloud, list rapidly on your paper (1) places you like, (2) where you think the student-author can add more, and

Neighbor Cake. Serves 8 to 10. Wonderful recipes are created when a cook finds out only an hour or so before supper that there will be one more mouth to feed. One of my favorites is [the Neighbor Cake], which gets its name from the fact that any ingredients you don't have in the house can easily be borrowed.

—Dori Sanders,
Dori Sanders' Country
Cooking, p. 205

Figure 4.1

THREE THINGS TO LISTEN FOR AT THE HELPING CIRCLE

1. Places you like
2. Places where the author can add more
3. Questions you still have

How it works:
1. One person reads his story (the reader). Everyone else is a listener and takes notes of the three things.
2. Listeners respond from their notes and the reader writes down the suggestions on his rough draft. (Questions are not answered aloud.)
3. Reader reads aloud the notes he took from the listeners. These are the things he will use in his revision.
4. Next person reads.

Figure 4.2

SIX THINGS TO LISTEN FOR AT THE HELPING CIRCLE

1. Places you like
2. Places where the author can add more
3. Questions you still have
4. Honesty
5. Voice
6. Mind pictures

How it works:
1. One person reads his story (the reader). Everyone else is a listener and takes notes of the six things.
2. Listeners respond from their notes and the reader writes down the suggestions on his rough draft. (Questions are not answered aloud.)
3. Reader reads aloud the notes he took from the listeners. These are the things he will use in his revision.
4. Next person reads.

(3) questions you still have. After the student has finished reading, hold up your own sloppy, scribbled notes and show them to students. Then respond from your notes while the student who read writes your comments on his rough draft, either inserted in the margins or as a list at the end.

When the second student volunteers to read aloud at the helping circle, tell all student listeners that they need to take notes in preparation for responding to the reader and that you will speak only after they have exhausted their comments. Let the process begin with the next reader, with everyone taking notes. After the author has read the paper aloud, students raise their hands for the author to call on them for their responses.

This is a time that always seems miraculous and magical to me. As students respond, you will strike items off your list. In almost all cases, student responders say everything you have written, and you will have nothing left to say. Together, when shown how, the students become the experts. Regardless of their age or ability level, students can help one another with their writing as well or better than the teacher can. How wonderful to put ourselves out of business! The helping circle allows students to show you (and themselves) what they can do.

With younger children, you may have to teach them how to take notes in a more detailed way. For example, 2nd graders and 3rd graders may have been practicing in class how to write complete sentences. When taking notes or writing classmates' suggestions, students may try to write complete sentences, a task that takes too long to make the helping circle a practical classroom strategy. Therefore, you need to teach students how to create their own form of shorthand by leaving out articles and other unnecessary words. With prekindergarten, kindergarten, and early 1st graders, much of the helping circle may be done aloud as students ease their way into writing on paper by raising their hands and responding aloud with questions and places they like. The response group can be oral, or the teacher may elect to write responses on the board, like dictation. Either way, these young students are following the practices used by successful writers—thus, learning how writers act and the ways they assist one another with writing.

After students have practiced responding at the helping circle, nominate a student to be the helping circle leader. At that time, you can move outside the circle and critique the helping circle process itself. At the end of the period, you may comment on their responses, their listening, and even their social skills as they help one another improve their writing.

When first teaching the helping circle, try letting students do full-class helping circles for two or three class sessions and then break them into smaller groups to finish. One advantage of moving to smaller circles is that students who are terrified of reading aloud can face a smaller audience. Another advantage is, of course, that a smaller group requires less class time. After students have become proficient at working in the smaller helping circles, it isn't usually necessary to use the full-class circle unless they need "a refresher course." Students are getting slack in their responses when they say, "We had a helping circle, and nobody could find anything wrong." Then you will know that it is necessary to have a whole-class helping circle to remind students of the responses and the procedure.

You may find it helpful to postpone reading rough drafts until after you have heard the students' papers read aloud at the helping circle. As teachers, we are trained to notice errors. Because we are distracted by these errors, we often miss the good story that is in the paper. During rough draft time, when students come to your desk to show you their paper and say, "How does this sound?" you may say, "Let me hear it at the helping circle first so that I can hear your story better." After they become familiar with the helping circle method, students adjust to everyone hearing the story before seeing it on paper.

Helping Circle Surprises

Here are some surprises I found when first teaching the helping circle in my classes.

◆ The purpose for writing changes. Writing becomes something kids have investment in; it is not just a school assignment. Calkins (1994) writes, "When students become deeply involved in their writing, they don't need motivating activities" (p. 11).

◆ Writing becomes something students care about. Like the practicing writers, students want to please their peer group. I have even had chronically absent students come to school especially to read at the helping circle.

◆ Questions like "How long does it have to be?" become non-existent. If a student writes something very short and then says, "I'm done!" you don't have to worry about it. When the student reads a

Never, never lie to yourself. Don't lie to others, but least of all to yourself.

—*Fyodor Dostoyevsky, in Brenda Ueland's,* If You Want to Write, *p. 137*

short or incomplete paper at the helping circle, classmates comment, "That's it?" and then ask the questions that bring out the rest of the story.

A student teacher recently wrote, "I think the students began to predict and foretell the types of questions and comments that the other students would have about their stories. This process helped them see the types of questions they needed to be asking themselves during the initial stages of writing." The questions that students predict as they write are signs of the same kinds of internal revision that adult authors use as they prepare to participate in writers' groups.

The Helping Circle in Action

Figures 4.3 (p. 74) and 4.4 (p. 76) demonstrate the helping circle at work in a 9th grade at-risk class and a 4th grade class. In Figure 4.3, the helping circle is led by a student.

The helping circle is a way to teach students of all ages how to write. An added benefit is that they are learning reading, speaking, listening, and social skills while they are learning how to improve their writing. In addition, the helping circle fosters compassion as students learn more about each other through their stories.

Letters from Teachers

Recently I received the following e-mail message from a teacher who attended one of my seminars:

> Last year I attended your seminar in the Pittsburgh area. At the
> time I was looking for suggestions to help motivate my students to
> write. What I discovered at the seminar was the concept of the
> helping circle. I thought that it was an amazing idea and hoped
> that I could incorporate it into my curriculum. I had to write to let
> you know how well this technique worked with my seventh graders.
> They were incredible at keying in on areas of a composition that

Figure 4.3
A STUDENT-LED HELPING CIRCLE

Chico (leader): Okay, who would like to go first?

Nicole: I will.

Chico: Okay, Nicole's going first. Everybody write down Nicole's name.

Nicole (reading): It was one warm morning when I did one crazy and funny thing. It all started when my mother combed my hair on one Thursday night. And I was in the fourth grade, and we was going on a field trip the next day, and I was so excited about that I didn't know how to act. I had to take my lunch, and I was so excited that I made my lunch that night before, and my mother ironed my clothes that night and laid them out. And she told me that she would do my hair in the morning. I was so excited that I felt butterflies in my stomach. That night my mother made my bath water, and she put lots of bubbles in it, and she took out my Mickey Mouse panties and my Mickey Mouse nightgown, and she bathed me. I remember awful well when she washed my hair and squeezed the rag over my head. I remember the words she used to say, "Hold in and close," and what she meant by that was hold my nose and close my eyes so that no water would get in. I used to love how she picked me up out the bathtub with a big towel with cartoon characters on it. That was my favorite towel. And when she used to pick me up out of the tub, she used to kiss me on my cheek.

I was so excited that I even went to bed early. I could barely sleep. It was just like on Christmas. The morning took so long to get here, and the reason why I was so excited was because we was going to Macon to visit a man who collected glass dolls.

So what happened was the morning finally got here, and my mother had to comb my hair, and when she combed it, I did not like it at all. She combed it in two pigtails and twisted it and put two bows at the end of it. And I just didn't like it. And at the time I had long hair, and my mother did also. At that particular time, she had on her nightclothes and bedroom shoes.

The bus was on the way up the road, and my mama kissed me good-bye. And in our house, we got two bathrooms, one across the hall from my bedroom and one in my Mama's bedroom. And there is a road right beside our house where the bus stops at. And when the bus stops it stops on that road. So when the bus stopped, I ran out the house like I was going to get on the bus, and I ran to the back glass door, the one my Mama gave me the key to, and I peeked in to see if she was in there. So then I peeked in the den to see was she there. And she wasn't. I looked all over the house, and I found out she was in her bathroom. So I ran in the bathroom across the hall from my room and got in the bathtub and shut the curtains and stood up in there. My Mama heard noises from the bathroom, and she came in the bathroom and looked around, and there she found me, in the bathtub, asleep. She spanked me with her bedroom shoe and took me on to school, and we got there in time before the bus left to go on our trip and before I got on the bus, my Mama said, I am going to have to explain why I missed the bus.

(continued)

Figure 4.3
(continued)

Chico: Would anyone like to make any comments about Nicole's paper?

Kesha: I like the part about the Mickey Mouse pajamas. (Nicole writes down what she says on her rough draft)

Semika: Yes, she had lots of good mind pictures.

Teacher: Which ones?

Marcus: The part about hold in and close.

James: Yea, man, that was good.

Jamie: I like the part about the favorite towel with the cartoon characters.

Kesha: The hiding in the bathtub.

Travis: How did you go to sleep that quick, or were you just pretending?

(Nicole continues to write. The focus is not the current discussion, but the paper itself. If there is a question, that means something which needs to be added to the paper.)

Mary Ann: It gets confusing to me about when it's night and when it's morning. Like, at the beginning you start off in the morning, and then it's night, and then you are fixing lunch the night before and . . . anyway, it gets confusing. Fix that part.

Travis: Yea, and make that part where she's starting to get on the bus and then she's peeping in the house to see where her mother is . . . that part is confusing too. Put in some more little details so it won't jump around so fast.

Loxie: Hey, man, that last part, that ending don't make no sense.

Tracy: Did you ever get to see the glass dolls?

(Nicole continues to write down what her classmates say, and the comments die down.)

Chico: Is there anything else for Nicole? Okay, read back what you've got.

Nicole (reading): likes the part about the Mickey Mouse pajamas, good mind pictures, likes part about hold in and close, likes part about towel with cartoon characters, likes hiding in the bathtub, did I go to sleep or was I pretending, confusing about night or daytime, fix that part about going back in the house, fix the ending, did I ever see the glass dolls.

Chico: Okay, who would like to read next?

—9th grade at-risk class

needed revision and, with very few exceptions, they focused on the same areas and had the same suggestions that I did. I could see the confidence that this technique gave them. They began to believe that they could write and that they could make their writing better by working together.

Figure 4.4
A 4TH GRADE HELPING CIRCLE

Mrs. Martin: Okay, who would like to read first?

Elizabeth: I will!

Mrs. Martin: Okay, everybody, Elizabeth is going to read first. Everybody write down Elizabeth's name.

Elizabeth (reading): When my brother got stitches. One day when our family went camping, my brother had to go to the bathroom, so he went alone. When he came back, his knee was bloody and cut open. The reason it got cut open is because it had just rained, and it was slippery and wet. He slipped on a rock; that's what he said anyway. His knee had a big hole, and it was bleeding really bad. My Mama and Daddy grabbed a big towel and wrapped it around Billy's knee real tight and put him on the back seat of the car. My Mama got in and sat beside him and they told me to get in the front. My daddy drove really fast to the hospital, and Billy got stitches in his knee. The End.

Mrs. Martin: Okay, now let's go around and tell Elizabeth what we liked about her story and any questions that we have. Marty?

Marty: I liked when you described his knee.

Alex: What things did you take camping? And what did you do with them when you left to go to the hospital?

(Elizabeth writes down the comments on her rough draft.)

Pete: Was your brother crying?

Mrs. Martin: Okay, Susan?

Susan: What was it like going to the hospital? Were you scared you were going to have a wreck since your daddy was driving so fast?

LouAnn: How many stitches?

Sharon: Where did you go camping?

Art: What did the camp site look like?

Chikita: Were there any other people there?

Lance: How is your brother's knee now?

Roxanne: Did you ever get to go back camping?

Ralph: I like where you said, "That's what he said anyway."

Chris: How old were you?

Mrs. Martin: Anybody else? Okay, Elizabeth, read back what you've got.

Elizabeth: Liked knee, what did we take, did Billy cry, were we scared, how many stitches, where go camping, how camp site look, how many people, how is knee now, ever get to go camping, liked what I said, how old was I.

Mrs. Martin: Okay, thank you, Elizabeth, now who would like to read next?

And this is a letter I received from a special education teacher who tried the helping circle in her classroom:

> My students' stories varied as much as my students—but the wondrous part came when we did the helping circle. The kids came up with such interesting ideas. They were taking notes, listening, and expanding their stories orally. I could not believe how much they wanted to talk about their stories and how closely they listened to each other read and even asked to re-read some parts. Our guidance counselor sat in and remarked that more was going on than just writing.

Prewriting Ideas for Teaching the Helping Circle

It's important for students to feel comfortable with the writing they are bringing to the helping circle. The following prewriting activities appear here rather than in the previous chapter because they are most effective in inspiring rough drafts to use for teaching students the process of the helping circle.

The childhood memory story is a good topic for a first-time experience with the helping circle. It helps students learn more about one another early in the process; therefore, they feel more comfortable about sharing their writing as the year progresses. The house story shows students how to tap into their own imaginations when creating writing. Both of these are almost foolproof as lesson plans, almost always producing good writing from students. After the childhood memory and the house story activities, you will find a few other prewriting activities that students will enjoy.

A Childhood Memory Story

Children think they have been living a long time and remember things that have happened to them. Only adults question whether young children have childhood memories. The childhood

It doesn't seem to matter if the house is large or small, guests who stay longer than an hour or two tend to end up in the kitchen.

—Dori Sanders,
Dori Sanders' Country Cooking, p. 192

memory story is my favorite assignment for helping students write a rough draft for the helping circle. Figures 4.5 (p. 79) and 4.6 (p. 80) contain sample prewriting sheets, one for older students and one for younger students. Here's how to start the process.

1. Using the appropriate prewriting sheets for your students, ask them to think of three childhood memories and to list them on the prewriting sheet as thoughts only (not writing out what happened). For example, "The time I learned to ride a bicycle" is a great childhood memory for the sheet. To help students understand the task, give them three examples from your childhood to help them get started. Students love to hear about *our* childhoods (they often think we were born old). Specifically identify the thought and phrase you'd write on the prewriting sheet and then you can elaborate on one or more to tell them a short story. Among others, I tell them about the time I punched my best friend, Candace (who was a bully), the time I found my Mr. Potato Head game sprouted in the closet (they learn that we had to use a real potato rather than a plastic one), and the time I got a spanking for climbing on the shoe shine stand in my Daddy's barber shop.

2. Then, working in pairs, students should tell each memory to their partner *in detail*. "Well, my friend and I were going to spend the day together, but when I got there, no one was home. I knocked and knocked and then went around to the back door and. . . ." Each partner should tell all three memories. This is a prewriting stage that I call "talking into writing," and it takes 15 to 20 minutes. Walk around the room and eavesdrop to encourage shy students to share. It is fun to hear students tell stories and to watch them as they gesture and to hear them make sound effects.

3. Each student should tell her partner which story she enjoyed most. Have each author circle that chosen story on the prewriting sheet. The story the student told with the most enthusiasm and detail will probably be the one she will write best.

4. Students should then brainstorm how to use the senses in their story. They should ask themselves what they see, hear, smell,

If you can discover what you truly believe about most of the major matters of life, you will be able to write a story which is honest and original and unique.

—Dorothea Brande, Becoming a Writer, p. 123

Figure 4.5
PREWRITING FOR OLDER STUDENTS

Name: _____ Class Period: _____ Date: _____

Topic: Childhood Memory

PreWriting

I. List three memories that you remember well from your childhood.

　　1. _____

　　2. _____

　　3. _____

II. Work with a partner for about 15 minutes. First, tell him about all three of your memories in detail. Ask him to determine which of your stories has the most detail and will make the best story. Then, listen as he tells you about his three memories and help him choose one of his stories—the one with the most detail to make the best story.

III. Brainstorming: Make a random list of all the details you can think of about this story. Think of sensual details—sights, sounds, smells, tastes, and things you feel in this story. Don't begin writing your story in sentences yet. Just make a list until you have exhausted your memory of the details.

_____

_____

_____

_____

_____

_____

_____

_____

_____

IV. Write the first two sentences of your story and read them to the class. Be sure what you write are really sentences and not a title. For example, "What happened to me on my fifth birthday" is a <u>title.</u> A <u>sentence</u> would be, "The day of my fifth birthday was a day I will never forget." (It has a subject and a verb and can stand on its own.)

First sentence:

_____

Figure 4.6
PREWRITING FOR YOUNGER STUDENTS

My Childhood Memory

1. _____

2. _____

3. _____

Senses in My Story

_____

_____

_____

The First Sentence of My Story

_____

_____

_____

---

taste, and touch in the story. "What sounds are in your story? What smells?" Students should list the senses in their story at the appropriate places on their prewriting sheets.

5. Before the end of class, get students to write the first one or two sentences of the chosen childhood memory. Then ask each student to read aloud just the first sentence. Reading aloud first sentences gives students the sense of sitting in a room filled with stories forming around them, and they can see how their story fits in with the others. They experience the suspense of wanting to know what is going to happen next in their classmates' stories. Students can write the rough draft at home or the next day in class, whichever is most appropriate.

The childhood memory activity almost always inspires good writing. Everyone enjoys the helping circle with these papers, and students are provided many opportunities to point out the good parts. This "talking into writing" idea can be used for opinion essays and many other kinds of writing (see "Essay from Memory Research" at the end of Chapter 7).

Figures 4.7 (p. 82) and 4.8 (p. 83) contain childhood memory stories from young writers. In "My Emus," the writer offers proof that even kindergarten children have childhood memories.

The House Story

This activity gives students an experience with creating their own stories. From *Southern Living, Better Homes and Gardens, House Beautiful, Architectural Digest*, or other similar magazines, cut out pictures of houses. The pictures should contain houses but no people. Mount the pictures on construction paper and laminate them for reuse. One good place to find house pictures is in calendars featuring the work of Thomas Kinkade. My pictures include a castle, an old shack, and a white house surrounded by flowers.

Give students a house prewriting sheet (see Figure 4.9, p. 84). Allow students to select a house picture from your collection, and tell them to look in the windows of the house they have chosen. Tell them to imagine the people in the house and to write a story about them. They have to include at least four characters, and something has to *happen* in their story. Don't be too concerned with the younger children creating conflict in their stories because the concept may be too advanced. If you choose a house, describe your characters, and make up a story on the spot, students can quickly understand the assignment.

Ask students to begin house stories by listing the names of the characters and their relationships to one another, the way a playwright lists characters at the beginning of a play. Students should list at least one activity for each character and an activity the character is performing in the house at the beginning of the story. The students can then let their imaginations take over and write their own story to find out what happens next.

The house story activity is always exciting because you can observe students actively engaged in the process of discovery as it

The process of the imagination is probably the most important part of the process of writing— and it is a part that has been virtually ignored by handbooks on composition.

—James E. Miller, Jr., and
    Stephen N. Judy,
Writing in Reality, p. 7

Figure 4.7
RITA'S PROBLEM

Once upon a Time, There was a little girl named Rita. She was nice To everyone. There was only one problem. She had never seen one of her grandmothers. She Thought about This problem all The Time. She had always known her American grandmother. But, you see, Rita was Afro-American, which means she was half African and half American. The Thought That Rita was missing out on another life in Africa disappointed her very much. Rita had never missed a year To send her grandmother a card on holidays.

Rita's dad knew how Rita felt about This matter. He soon started saving $200 out of each paycheck. Rita also had been saving money. Soon They had saved enough money To go and visit Rita's grandmother.

Rita was anxious and eager To go and see her grandmother. As Rita and her dad boarded The ship, a feeling of joy came over her. It Took several days To reach Africa. Rita and her dad Then had To Travel To Nigeria and from There To Lagos and Then To Benin. Rita was surprised To see how beautiful Africa was.

Rita and her dad soon caught a cab. All Rita's dad said was "Omobude," and The driver started driving. They soon reached a small village. It had a large farm outside of it. Rita's dad Then got out of The car To meet an old woman. She hugged him and kept shouting out something That Rita couldn't quite understand but

(continued)

Figure 4.7
(continued)

Thought she was saying "Richard." Rita soon got out of the car to see what this old woman would do. She came over to Rita and grabbed her to hug. Rita knew then that she was her grandmother.

Rita and her dad had parades, feasts, dance contests and so many other things. Soon it was time to go. Everyone gave them going-away presents. They boarded the ship and returned home. Not long after that, Rita received a letter. It said, "I am happy that I got to meet you. You were everything I expected and more. I will never forget you. Even when I'm dead, I'll still remember you. PS I am dying, but don't be sad. You met me once."

Rita wasn't sad at all but happy that she did see her grandma.

—Rita Omobude, 5th grade

Figure 4.8
MY EMUS

When I ws 5 yrs old I got 4 Emos. I namd thm Sara, Dukie, Petree and Litleut. I lik to klim the fins and feed them. SumTims the pek me. Mommy sqirts us with a watr hos. 1 day Sara and Dukie ran away. Thay ran fast like ostrigs. Now I hav 2 The End

—Ashley Marie Avant, Kindergarten

Figure 4.9
PREWRITING SHEET FOR THE HOUSE STORY

Characters (List people in the house)	Location (Where is each person?)	Occupation (What is each person doing?)
1.		
2.		
3.		
4.		

Make a note regarding relationships among characters—parents, grandparents, siblings, friends. Write the rough draft of your story on notebook paper. It can be messy—it's a rough draft!

takes over the classroom. Students lose control as their pencils run away with them when the creative process takes over. They discover the tremendous power of their own imagination.

Once I was using this activity with a rowdy 9th grade class—the kind you have to keep the lid on. In the middle of the activity, someone came to the door with an emergency and called me into the hallway. When I went back into the room, I expected to find the whole class completely off-task. Instead, what I found was a room of students, each consumed by imagination. The room was filled with the sound of pencils scratching on paper. I felt as if I could *hear* the stories being created.

Students working on the house story have even asked "Does it matter how long we make it?" which is a very different question from "How long does it have to be?" Students who have never been very interested in writing before look up from their papers, grin, and say, "You're going to like this story!"

Denise's house story, Figure 4.10, is one of my favorite examples of this activity. This story is exactly as she wrote it, errors and all.

Figure 4.10
DENISE'S HOUSE STORY

Once upon of Time IT was a big brown raggedy rusty house sitting way ouT in a pasTor, in ThaT house was a liTTle old lady name Mae. And in The house she had one bed and also her dog Jim and on The ouTside of The house she had no windows almosT no doors. A black raggedy skeelybug look like IT never been crank. And way way down The oTher side of The pasTor was Two more people ThaT was a lady and a man ThaT sTayed in a barn, and There name, were Lucy and BoBo, They had noThing To live for, They use To come visiT Mae all The Time, buT see, Mae didn'T have any food To eaT excepT liTTle sTuff ouT in The yard.

BuT one day Lucy and BoBo came To visiT her wiTh a big kroker sack in Their arm. IT was a kroker sack full of differenT kind of vegeTables.

Mae was very happy To see The food. She was all dancing around in her long granny dress old Jim was barking and Lucy and BoBo was very hap To.

Every one gaThered around Mae's one bed where They had puT The food and They all had a wonderful feasT.

—Denise

Source: From "Five Good Writing Ideas," by S. Worsham, May‑June 2000, *Teachers and Writers*, X, pp. 9‑12. Adapted with permission.

Remember that these are rough drafts in the early stages of the writing process and not final copies ready to be published.

Car Story

This is a variation of the house story activity. Have students cut out pictures of cars, trucks, motorcycles, or any other vehicles from magazines. Next, have them fill out a prewriting sheet telling about the drivers and riders in their vehicle, where they have been, and where they are going. Then they should write a story about the people. Figure 4.11 (p. 87) contains a 1st grade car story.

Stories from Picture Combinations

As you peruse old magazines, cut out pictures of people and animals. Laminate the pictures for use in your classroom and store them in a box. Tell each student to blindly select three pictures and to write a story that contains those three characters. Students should give their characters names and decide the characters' relationships to one another. For example, a student may take out a picture of a stern-looking elderly man, a young woman running across a field, and a golden retriever puppy sitting in a basket. The student may decide to write a story called, "The Puppy Whose Mommy Ran Away." The interesting thing about this activity is that the combinations are always different, no matter how many times you use the same set of pictures. Like Forrest Gump's box of chocolates, "You never know what you're gonna get" (Finerman, Newirth, Starkey, & Tisch, 1994).

Stories from Catalog People

I got this idea from my own childhood game of cutting people out of catalogs and making up stories about them. Using catalogs or magazines that contain pictures of people, let students cut out their own characters and make up a story about them. It is interesting to watch children do this because they begin making up their story as they are cutting out the characters. For example, they will cut out

It is important to read aloud what you write. In writing groups, I ask people to write and then immediately afterward ask them to read it to either the large group, a smaller group, or to a person sitting next to them. It is part of the writing process, like bending down to touch your toes and then standing up again. . . . I don't know quite what this reading aloud is about, but we tend to get swampy, thick with sludge, when we write. We listen too much to monkey mind. Reading aloud gives us an airing.

—Natalie Goldberg,
Wild Mind: Living the Writer's Life, p. 81–82

Figure 4.11
MOTORCYCLE STORY

Chris, Ed, and Kim are going To The mouTains in a moTorcycle. The moTorcycle is blue and silver. I goT iT aT my birThday parTey.

—1sT grade

---

the character and then they will cut out the character's car, food, and house.

Revision

Revision is difficult to teach because students often feel that their story is complete the first time. They don't understand what is supposed to *happen* in revision, so they don't know what to do. But the helping circle teaches students to *like* revision because it helps them know what to do when they revise. Revision means *re-vision,* or seeing your writing again. Sol Stein (1999) quotes Bernard Malamud on revision, "'First drafts . . . are for learning what your novel or story is about. Revision is working with that knowledge to enlarge and enhance an idea, to re-form it'" (p. 150). In *The Writers Chapbook,* Malamud says, "Revision is one of the true pleasures of writing" (Plimpton, 1989, p. 130).

As students revise their papers, have them insert the notes from the helping circle at the appropriate places in the improved story. They should write their revision copy neatly enough for their classmates to read it when they get to the proofreading step. Tell students if they can think of ways to make their paper better as they revise, things not suggested by their classmates, to go ahead and make those changes. As Henry Miller says in *Writers at Work,* "When I'm revising, I use a pen and ink to make changes, cross out, insert. The manuscript looks wonderful afterwards, like a Balzac. Then I retype, and in the process of retyping, I make more changes" (Plimpton, 1963, p. 170).

Students also have the right to disagree with their classmates' suggestions. I tell them to make their paper longer and better and to use the suggestions from the helping circle, along with their own ideas. As students revise, they discover things. Like writers of any age, they rearrange sentences; they lengthen; they delete; they add examples. Revision still does not mean proofreading or aiming for correct spelling, grammar, usage, and mechanics. It means focusing and learning where the writing is leading. "See revision," Goldberg (1991a) writes, "as 'envisioning again.' If there are areas in your work where there is a blue or vagueness, you can simply see the picture again and add the details that will bring your work closer to your mind's picture" (p. 165).

Steps for Revising

This is a quick overview of the revision process for students:

◆ Insert helping circle suggestions on your rough draft.

◆ Put the rough draft on one side of the desk and clean paper on the other side.

◆ Rewrite your paper, making it better and longer, using the suggestions from the helping circle, plus other ideas you think of yourself.

Ricardo, Master of Revision

I taught Ricardo in a basic level class when he was in the 10th grade. Before Ricardo was actually in my class, I had already heard of him. He was known throughout school as a troublemaker. He talked back to teachers, he skipped school, and he was suspended many times.

I had already learned that students who need extra amounts of peer-group attention often make good helping circle leaders, and

I always show my work to one or two people before sending a copy to my editor or agent. I feel more secure and connected this way, and these two people get a lot of good work out of me. They are like midwives; there are these stories and ideas and visions and memories and plots inside me, and only I can give birth to them. Theoretically I could do it alone, but it sure makes it easier to have people helping.

—Anne Lamott,
Bird by Bird, *p. 164*

this proved to be true of Ricardo. He kept the circle moving and made perceptive comments about other students' writing. When it came time for revision, he used the suggestions his classmates made to improve his paper. He added the details they suggested to create better images.

Ricardo's revisions were so striking that I took one of his papers with me to the NCTE convention in Baltimore that year and shared it with other English teachers. This paper and its revisions are featured as Figures 4.12 (p. 90) and 4.13 (p. 93). To better understand the changes Ricardo made, try to find someone to read aloud the revised copy while you follow along on the rough draft. Or, better yet, read aloud the revised copy in class while your students follow along on the rough draft. That way, you can *show* them how to revise their writing.

Proofreading

In the proofreading stage, each student gets three other students to read his paper. Up to this point, all papers have been heard, not read, and all responses have been made aloud. In the proofreading stage, however, student editors pretend to be the English teacher and make comments directly on the classmate's revision copy. The student editors correct mechanics and other errors. Three colors of felt-tipped pens for each paper helps identify the editors and allows for follow-up if students are not reading or proofreading carefully. In the upper right corner of the revision, ask the editors to sign their names with the felt-tipped markers.

Proofreading is a time for learning language conventions in a real way and for real reasons. Chan Edwards, a 3rd grader, is an exceptional proofreader. Her classmates line up, waiting for her to proof their paper. One thing that is especially impressive about Chan—a budding English teacher, I predict—is that she doesn't just make corrections, she also explains the changes to her classmates.

Figure 4.12
RICARDO'S ROUGH DRAFT

The Time I Lost My Dog, Killer

It was a hot, sunny day when I decided to go out and play with my dog, Killer. Killer was a white bulldog that loved to play a lot. I named him Killer because sometimes when we played he would act kinda mean. I was about six years old and short. My nose used to run all the time so I used to keep all four pockets full of tissue. I remember going outside that day with some cut off blue jeans, a black shirt with a hole in the sleeve, no socks, and a pair of wildcat Tennis shoes. As I was going out of the door I heard Grandma yell, don't go any further than the yard because I'm baking cookies. And another thing. You and Killer stay away from that road. So I yelled, yes, ma'am and went on my way to the back yard where Killer was tied up. I was going to be sure that I stayed around the house because I loved grandmas chocolate chip cookies. So I untied Killer and we began to roll around on the grass and play. I could tell how he jumped on me and knocked me down he was glad to be untied. As we played I heard some loud yelling coming from next door. It was Mr. and Mrs. O'Neal our next door neighbors arguing again. Mr. O'Neal was a short bald man and he loved to talk. Mrs. O'Neal was also short and had beautiful black hair. But I knew that the hair was a wig because I went over there early one morning for my grandma. I knocked on the door and she came and it was twisted to one side

(continued)

Figure 4.12
(continued)

and underneath were some little gray plats of hair. So I gave
her The message and as soon as she closed The door I laughed
myself To death. So anyway They were arguing again as usual.
They were saying some preTTy bad words. AfTer a while of lis-
Tening To ThaT I wenT back To playing wiTh Killer because The
words goT To rough for me. Soon after we sTop rolling on The
ground we sTarTed playing chase. I chased Killer in The fronT yard
forgeTTing grandma said sTay away from The road. Then I goT ouT
of breath and sTopped running. I called Killer To come back buT
he KepT going. Killer, Killer, I yelled buT he never Turned around.
Then iT happened he ran inTo The road and juST as he goT inTo
The road This big long gray LTD came flying over The hill and
hiT Killer, seeing This I ran inTo The road hoping he was O.K.
The car KepT going and never sTopped. I shook him and called his
name buT he didn'T bark or move, very upseT and my eyes full
of Tears, I Told my grandma whaT happened, so she ran ouT and
looked. Then she Told me Killer was gone. I said no he isn'T he's
lying in The road. She said no I mean dead you'll never see him
again. I cried even worse Then. Grandma hugged me and Told me
iT was going To be okay. So I wenT and lay down on The bed
and KepT crying. I lifTed my head eyes full of Tears and noTiced
grandma dialing The phone. ThaT wasn'T imporTanT so I lay my
head back down and conTinued crying. AbouT Ten minuTes laTer I
heard a loud noise ouTside so I goT off The bed and wiped my

(continued)

Figure 4.12
(continued)

face and went out on the porch. I looked out in the road next to Killer There was a man standing next to a big Truck with a pair of dirty blue jeans and a red plaided shirt on with a old rusty shovel in his hand. I had no idea what he was going To do. Then he shoveled up Killer and Threw him on the back of the Truck got in and drove off. I still remember That day and every since That happened I've been scared To ask for another dog.

—Ricardo BranTley

Some students have a natural talent for proofreading and are in demand during the proofreading stage. Their explanations and corrections help other students learn to proofread well.

Watch students carefully during proofreading because they will try to do it too quickly. The proofreading stage, not before, is the time to review and study mechanics. When writers become concerned with proofreading early in their writing—in the rough draft stage, for example—ideas are stifled and thoughts don't flow.

Again, consider the way successful writers write. Many famous writers are poor spellers, but they do not concentrate on usage and mechanics and correctness until the final stage, prior to publishing. They know better than to interrupt the creative flow. At the proofreading stage, tell students that this is the time for correctness. Tell them that you, the teacher, are now the editor-in-chief and that errors in the paper will be reflected in the final grade. If a paper comes to you with mechanic and usage errors, tell students to make better use of their proofreaders. Students take the proofreading step more seriously if they know you check behind them and that the final grade is affected by any remaining errors.

Figure 4.13
RICARDO'S REVISION

The Time I Lost My Dog, Killer

It was a hot sunny day when I decided to go out and play with my dog, Killer. Killer was a white bulldog that loved to play a lot. I named him Killer because sometimes when we played he'd act kinda mean and snap at my finger. I was about six years old and short. My nose used to run all the time, so I used to keep all four pockets full of tissue. I remember I was getting ready to go outside. I had on some cut-off blue jeans, a black shirt with a hole in the sleeve, no socks, a pair of wildcat tennis shoes, and—you guessed it—all four pockets stuffed with Charmin bathroom tissue.

As I headed for the door I heard Grandma yell in a very loud pitched voice, "Don't go any farther than the back yard because I'm baking cookies. And another thing, you and Killer stay away from that road."

So I yelled, "Yes, Ma'am" and went on my way to the back yard where Killer was tied up against an old tall oak tree with a big piece of bark scraped off the side.

I was going to be sure that I stayed around the house because I loved Grandma's chocolate chip cookies. All I could see were visions of those big, delicious, chocolate chips, surrounded by that soft chewy outside that melted in my mouth.

So after the visions finally disappeared, I untied Killer, and we began to roll around and play on the grass. I could tell how he jumped on me and knocked me down he was glad to be untied.

(continued)

Figure 4.13
(continued)

As we played, I heard some loud yelling coming from next door. It was Mr. and Mrs. O'Neal, our next door neighbors arguing again. Mr. O'Neal was a short bald man that wore a Sears and Roebuck blue jean overall outfit every day, and he loved to talk. Mrs. O'Neal was also short but a little taller than Mr. O'Neal and had beautiful black hair. But I knew that the hair was a wig because I went over to their house early one Saturday morning running an errand for my Grandma. I knocked on the door, and she came to the door wearing a white gown covered with coffee stains and some old burgundy slippers with a hole in the left one. I noticed that the wig was twisted to one side and underneath were some little gray plaits of hair mixed with lint. I gave her the message, and as soon as she closed the door, I laughed myself to death on the way back home. So, anyway, they were going at it again saying some terrible things to each other.

After a while of listening to that, I went back to playing with Killer because the language was too rough. Soon after, we stopped rolling on the ground, and we started playing chase. I chased Killer in the front yard forgetting Grandma said to stay away from the road. Then I stopped, out of breath, and pulled some tissue from my back pocket and wiped my nose. I called Killer to come back, but he never turned around.

"Killer! Killer!" I yelled, but still no response. Then it happened. He ran into the road, and just as he entered, this big long gray Ford LTD came flying over the hill, and within seconds Killer was hit.

(continued)

Figure 4.13

(continued)

I ran inTo The road hoping he was okay. The car kepT going and never sTopped. I shook Killer and called his name, buT he didn'T bark or move.

Very upseT and my eyes full of Tears, I ran up The sTeps, Through The screen door, and Told my Grandma whaT had happened. So she ran ouT and looked. Then she said, "Killer is gone."

I said, "No, he isn'T. He's lying in The road."

She said, "No, Baby, I mean dead. You'll never see him again."

I cried even worse Then. Grandma hugged me TighT and Told me iT was going To be all righT. So we wenT back inTo The house, and I wenT and laid down on The bed and kepT crying. I lifTed my head, my eyes full of Tears, and noTiced Grandma dialing The phone. ThaT wasn'T imporTanT, so I laid my head back down and conTinued crying.

AbouT Ten minuTes laTer, I heard a loud noise coming from ouTside. So I goT off The bed, wiped my face with my lasT piece of Tissue from my pockeT, and wenT on The porch where my Grandma was sTanding. I looked ouT in The road nexT To Killer, and There was a kind of sTouT man sTanding nexT To a big whiTe dump Truck with wriTing on The side. He was wearing a pair of dirTy blue jeans, a red plaid shirT, and had a cigar in his mouTh and a rusTy shovel in his hand. I had no idea whaT he was going To do. Then he shoveled up Killer, Threw him on The back of The Truck along with The shovel, waved aT my Grandma, goT in, and drove off. Then The only memory I had of Killer was ThaT big bloodsTain in The middle of The road.

(continued)

Figure 4.13

(continued)

I was still upset as Grandma and I walked back in the house. As we walked up the steps, I said, "Grandma, who was that man?"

She said, "He was from the sanitation department."

"Who?"

"Sorta like a trash man with a different truck."

I said, "Oh, he's going to throw Killer away?"

She said, "I'm afraid so."

I was still Kind of upset. Then we entered the house, and Grandma said, "I smell smoke." We raced to the kitchen, and Grandma said, "I forgot about the cookies during all this confusion."

She opened up the stove, and all I saw were some little black things on a pan smoking. She said, "I'm afraid I'm going to have to throw them out."

And ever since that day, I've been afraid to ask for another dog because I figured he'd get Killed, or my cookies would burn up.

—Ricardo Brantley

Source: Adapted with permission from the 1992 *Rain Dance Review*, published by Baldwin High School.

We need to be sure students understand the importance of correctness when their writing will be seen by others. Writers want their writing to impress, move, influence, and enlighten their readers. Above all, they want to communicate. Writers strive for correct products, not so much because people criticize errors or they'll get a bad grade, but because their readers—their audience—may misunderstand the writing and it will not serve the purpose or have the effect they intend.

Proofreading Steps for Students

◆ Indicate three places for proofreaders' signatures on the top right corner of the revision copy.

◆ Find three proofreaders to review your copy. Ask the proofreaders to sign their names after proofreading and to pass the copy along to the next proofreader. (A box of pens with colored ink on the teacher's desk allows each proofreader to select his own color.)

◆ Check to ensure the paper has been proofread carefully by all three proofreaders and compare corrections with signatures.

Final Copy

The final copy must be as close to perfect as students can make it in preparation for publication, with the proofreaders' changes incorporated. The paper must be written in ink, front side only, and double-spaced, or it may be printed from a computer (double spaced). The extra space between the lines gives the student editors room to make corrections and comments. By this time, the students have had many chances to polish their papers through peer response, revision, and proofreading. They have used the steps followed by serious writers in preparation for publication, the final stage in the writing process. Therefore, the teacher's job of grading these papers is greatly facilitated.

Summary

The helping circle is a magical and amazing tool for teaching students to write. To convince teachers, I can only say to try it and watch students shine. The childhood memory and the house story assignments are reliable prewriting activities for getting rough drafts to use at the helping circle. Revision, long a source of loud complaining, becomes the natural next step and one students want to move to after receiving feedback from their peers. As students

Good writers meet their readers only at their best. If you should read the sentences in their wastebaskets, you would find them full of bad starts and complete misses. When you write, you can discard your bad tries and forget them.

—Ken Macrorie,
Telling Writing, p. 25

learn to respond at the helping circle and move toward the final copy and publication, they become practicing writers who care about their writing. They care, not because they are trying to please the teacher or get a grade but because they are trying to please themselves and their audience. Student writing becomes something that matters for its own sake.

Chapter 5 finishes the writing process by suggesting exciting and unique ways to publish student writing.

Suggestions for the Teacher

◆ Write your own childhood memory story with students and read it aloud to them.

◆ Use the helping circle and discuss with students how it worked. Share the idea with your colleagues.

◆ Ask your most troublesome student to lead the helping circle.

Mama's Candied Sweet Potatoes

4 or 5 medium sweet potatoes   *salt to taste*   *white sugar*   *1 pat of butter (optional)*

◆ In a large pot filled with water, boil the sweet potatoes in their skins until tender (about 45 minutes). Pour off the water and store the potatoes in the refrigerator overnight.

◆ The next day, preheat the oven to 375°; peel the potatoes (the skins just fall off) and slice into half-inch slices, lengthwise. Place a single layer in a 9" × 14" glass baking dish. Sprinkle lightly with salt. Completely cover the potato slices with a heavy blanket of white sugar. Repeat the layers (usually 2 layers of each ingredient). When this dish is ready for the oven, the sugar covers the potatoes so much that the orange doesn't show through. Dot top with butter (optional).

◆ Bake 45 minutes or until the top looks candied. The secrets to this recipe: don't add any water and be very generous with the sugar!

Exploring Publishing Options

5

THIS RECIPE WAS MAMA'S SPECIALTY FOR AS LONG AS I CAN REMEMBER. She always took candied sweet potatoes to covered dish dinners at church. Family and friends would tell her, "I followed your directions exactly, but mine never tastes like yours." Mama enjoyed the recognition and praise she received from this, her specialty dish.

The secret to this recipe is to use lots and lots of white sugar (no brown sugar); use so much sugar that the color of the potatoes is covered. During cooking, the sugar melts into syrup and makes a wonderful juice to sop the potatoes around in. The sweet potato flavor, the bright orange color, and the sweet smell are a feast for the senses and an important part of my childhood memories of my mother's kitchen.

We all enjoy feeling special and receiving recognition and praise. For writers, publishing means getting special recognition, being known for something, and even feeling famous. That's true whether the writer is a previously published author or an elementary school student. A student in special education, when published in the literary magazine, asked his father, "Does this mean that I am famous?"

What Publishing Can Do

One of my favorite examples of what publishing can do for students happened a year or so ago when I was away from school

Mother, in an orgy of baking brought on probably by all the beautiful eggs and butter lying around, spent every Saturday morning making cakes. . . . They were filled with crushed almonds, chopped currants, and an outrageous number of calories. They were beautiful. Saturday afternoons they sat cooling, along with Mother and the kitchen after the hectic morning, and by Sunday night they were already a pleasant if somewhat bilious memory.

—MFK Fisher,
The Art of Eating, *p. 366*

giving a workshop. The plan I left for the substitute was for the students to write "The Happiest Thing That Ever Happened to Me." When I returned, I found among the papers a piece by Shari (Figure 5.1), a student whose essay we had mailed to the *Union-Recorder* as a letter to the editor.

The result of this assignment was an eye opener for me. Usually teenagers pick "the time I got my new CD player" or "the time my baby sister was born." But this student chose publication as her happiest thing—what a superlative for publishing!

Like Shari, I remember when I was first published—I was in 3rd grade. My teacher, Mrs. Rogers, typed my poem, "The Baby," and ran it off on the old purple mimeograph machine.

> *The student of writing who does not publish what he writes can be compared with the athlete who never gets into a game. The act of writing is not complete until a piece of writing is published and read, and the teacher should seek whatever ways he can in his own school to achieve a variety of publication for his students.*
>
> *—Donald Murray,* A Writer Teaches Writing, *p. 162*

The Baby

Look at the baby

Lying in bed.

Isn't he cute?

Just look at his head.

Figure 5.1
THE HAPPIEST THING THAT EVER HAPPENED TO ME

The happiest Thing That ever happened To me is when my article goT published in The newspaper. I was so happy. I didn'T really know iT was in The newspaper unTil my grandmoTher called me and Told me congraTulaTions. Then I asked her whaT she was Talking abouT, and she Told me ThaT my article was in The newspaper. I said, "You for real?" Then she said, "Yes." Then she said ThaT she was very proud of me. And The principal announced my name on The inTercom aT school.

—Shari, 9Th grade

More than 40 years later I not only remember that little poem, but also that feeling of awe when Mrs. Rogers put into my hands my published poem. It was just a mimeographed sheet, but to me it was like *The New York Times*. Think what power we have as teachers that we can do something for students that they will remember when they are older than we are now.

In the seven-step writing process that practicing writers most often use, prewriting, the helping circle, and publishing are the most motivating steps. Of these three, however, publication is probably the most exciting for students. Publication is that experience that gets writers of all ages and levels hooked on writing.

Practicing writers place a high premium on publication. Until publication, they may call themselves writers, but their writing lacks a certain respect and legitimacy. "Where have you published?" is one of the first questions editors ask.

Publishing for our students, however, has a broader definition than being published in a literary magazine, a newspaper, or a book. Publishing is any method of sharing a student's work with others. There are many ways to publish student work. Figure 5.2 (p. 104) lists some of them, and others are discussed in more detail this chapter.

Literary Magazines

One natural way to publish student work is in a school literary magazine. The *Rain Dance Review* at Baldwin High School in Milledgeville, Georgia, publishes all ability levels of students, from the very gifted to those students enrolled in special education. Each spring, the school has a reception and autograph party honoring the students whose work is published in the magazine. At the reception, the school's drama department presents their interpretations of the works in the magazine. In addition, the student staff members of the magazine visit elementary and middle schools throughout the county to share the magazine and conduct writing workshops with younger children. In this way, the young writers become writing teachers and temporary mentors. Elementary

My mother was a hungry woman. She related to food with a sensuality which disguised and fended off deeper yearnings she could not name.

—*Clare Coss,*
"My Mother/Her Kitchen,"
Through the Kitchen Window,
p. 13

Figure 5.2
SELECT WAYS TO PUBLISH

Publishing can take many forms and can be a very creative way to challenge the writers in your classroom and to celebrate writing. Choose from among these ideas to fit your students, resources, and talent.

- Bookmaking
- Read aloud on the intercom
- Sponsor readings in the school auditorium
- Read aloud in the classroom
- Videotape and mail readings of student writing to another classroom in another school, across town, or across the country
- Write books for other grades, younger or older
- Hold an author's autograph party
- Make a class anthology
- Hang papers on a clothesline across the room
- Post papers on the wall outside the classroom
- Enter papers in contests
- Mail essays and letters to the local newspaper
- Mail student writing to parents
- Designate an author's chair
- Make pop-up books
- Make bookmarks with a student's favorite quote from his own writing
- Make shape books (e.g., things "deer" to me)
- Write and decorate monthly journals
- Make flip books (like a flip chart)
- Create accordion books (fold like an accordion and write the story on the sections)
- Translate a story into a mobile or a windsock
- Copy a story on an overhead transparency
- Celebrate author's day by inviting parents to see displays of student work and to hear students read their work
- Take a day and publish a class book
- Select an Author of the Week and feature work on the intercom and on a bulletin board
- Use a publishing program to create a class newsletter or a student brochure and send copies to the public library, hospitals, and nursing homes
- Publish on the Internet

teachers use the childhood memory stories in the magazine as story ideas and reading material for their students.

One of the most meaningful outcomes of the literary magazine is that reluctant writers have been published. I remember one of these reluctant writers, Henry, coming into my classroom and pulling his wadded acceptance slip from his pocket to show me. I remember the students signing autographs at the reception. These students will not be honored because of scholarship or skill in sports, but this publication experience is something real and tangible. They can talk about it and show it to their children and grandchildren. They can relish the memory and enjoy the present, for publication is something they can hold in their hands.

The story in Figure 5.3, one of my favorites, was written by a student classified as at-risk. The night of the literary magazine reception, I saw my mother congratulate the author and tell her that she especially liked her story about her mother's dishes. The student beamed; her joy was evident in her face.

The Literary Magazine Across the Curriculum

The literary magazine is not just for the writing the students do in English class. Teachers and students can submit good writing,

---

Figure 5.3
CHRISTMAS WISH

My Christmas wish is to buy my mother a pretty set of dishes. Some of her dishes are broken. She really wants new dishes like the ones she saw in the Family Dollar sale paper. I'm doing cleaning work to pay for them.

My mother is good to us. She gives us her last pennies. She works hard cooking, cleaning, and washing our clothes.

I am making her a present in Industrial Arts class, but I still want to buy her new dishes. She will be surprised, and that makes me very happy.

—Sandra Waller, 10th grade

Source: Published in the 1987 *Rain Dance Review* by Baldwin High School. Used with permission.

regardless of the discipline. The *Rain Dance Review* has published titles including "Life of a Snail," "I Believe in Atoms," and "Einstein's Dream" by science students; "Image Reaction to *Pachelbel's Canon in D Major*" and "A Few Extra Beats in Band" by music students; "Wrestling a Blind Person" from the physical education department; and "Dedication to the EMT" by a health occupations student. In addition, the foreign languages department publishes poems in Spanish and French.

The literary magazine venue offers a source of materials for elementary, middle, and high school teachers in all disciplines. Foreign language teachers use samples for students to read and comprehend, and English teachers use the samples for teaching essay writing. The world history teacher in our county uses the essay in Figure 5.4 (p. 107) when students study communism.

A school literary magazine is a wonderful way to make writing an important part of a school. Many schools have literary magazines, but you can expand the scope of them to strengthen the writing program by publishing all ability levels, not just advanced students; assigning staff members to visit other schools and conduct writing activities while sharing the publication; hosting a reception and autograph party to celebrate each new issue; and publishing writing from all subject areas.

The Celebration of Writing

Another way to publish student writing is through a county-wide writing contest. In Milledgeville, we call our contest the Celebration of Writing. This program can be conducted in any city and is a wonderful way to create awareness about the importance of writing in your community.

The contest involves all classrooms in our county. The three winners from each classroom receive a certificate and are entered into grade-level competition. Each grade-level winner receives a T-shirt that reads, "A Celebrated Writer" on the front and lists corporate sponsors on the back. Each county-level winner is awarded a

Feeling low, I yearned after one of those soft puddly custards or cool puddings I was fed as a child . . . and asked myself about the solace these humble, almost austere dishes offer.

—Judith Moore,
Never Eat Your Heart Out,
p. 241

Figure 5.4
LIFE UNDER A COMMUNIST GOVERNMENT

Freedom. A word most people take for granted. They don't think twice about it, because here in the United States, they are free to do whatever they please without having to worry about the government watching every word they say and every move they make.

If you were to ask me what I am most thankful for, it would definitely be freedom, because unfortunately I was born and lived under a communist government for seven years. The story that I am about to tell is one you probably won't believe unless you lived in it.

First of all, most people don't know what Communism means. Communism is a system in which the government has total control over businesses, enterprises, politics, the economy, and the people themselves. The people have no control whatsoever. The government tells you what to do, when to do it, where you can work, where you can live, and when you can go shopping. The government tells you how much you can buy in the way of food, clothing, toys, and other things.

I was born in Havana, Cuba, in 1966. Castro, the president of Cuba, had taken over in 1959. Castro is the head of the government. He is the one who started Communism in Cuba.

In 1968, my daddy asked permission for my family to leave Cuba and come here to the United States. Back then, if you wanted to leave the country, you had to ask permission from the

(continued)

Figure 5.4
(continued)

government, and Then government officials could keep you waiting for as long as They pleased before They let you go.

Finally, after six years, in 1974, They gave us permission To leave. Waiting Those six years was like living in prison, if not worse. First, shopping is not like it is here in The United States, where if you have The money, you can buy whatever you want. In Cuba, The government gives you a quota card. This is like a little notebook where The government allows you To buy only a certain amount and kind of products. For example, if you went shopping in a shoe store, The card would say how many pairs of shoes To buy, and how much They cost; and Those are The only kind That you can buy. If you went To The store, and The shoes which The card said were gone, Then you could not buy another pair of shoes, probably for The next five months. The same goes for clothes and food. I remember my mother waiting in line in grocery stores for hours. Sometimes you would even have To spend The night There just To get something To eat. You could only get meat once a month, if you were lucky. Most of The Time, you would just have To eat eggs.

Children under six years of age and adults over sixty-five are The only ones who can drink milk. Once you Turn seven, you no longer have Toys. In Cuba, we don't celebrate Christmas, and The only Time all year That children get Toys is in July, which is The

(continued)

Figure 5.4
(continued)

Anniversary of The Revolution, and The children are allowed only Three Toys during ThaT Time. You cannoT go To The sTore and buy any more during The year.

All schools belong To The governmenT, and The educaTion is free. Children go To school unTil They are eleven. Once They Turn Twelve, They have To go and work in The counTry, doing whaTever iT is The governmenT wanTs Them To do. The children are separaTed from Their parenTs several Times a year when They go off To work in The counTry.

All newspapers, Television, radio sTaTions, and movie indusTries belong To The governmenT. EveryThing you see and read has To do wiTh The governmenT. There are no programs on Television or aT The movies ThaT are comedy, drama, or mysTery. They all have To do wiTh governmenT. Finally, There is in each block a house in Which people from The governmenT live. These people are assigned To keep an eye on everyThing you do. They know where you work, where you go, who your friends are, and who comes To your house To visiT. If They suspecT someThing wrong, They will reporT iT To The police and puT you in prison. In Cuba, you can easily go To prison jusT for saying one bad word abouT The governmenT, because There is no freedom of speech.

Even Though I was only seven years old when I lefT The counTry, I've experienced someThing which I will never forgeT. And

(continued)

Figure 5.4

(continued)

even Though I was Too young To undersTand exacTly whaT was happening, I knew ThaT whaTever was going on, I didn'T like iT. I wanTed To geT away from ThaT Terrible counTry and come here To The UniTed STaTes. I remember my moTher and faTher always Telling me how wonderful iT was up here and how we would never have To worry abouT Communism ever again.

While leaving The counTry was The besT Thing ThaT ever happened To my family and me, iT was also one of The worsT. We had To leave The resT of my family behind, noT knowing wheTher we would ever see Them again. When we lefT Cuba, we had To leave everyThing. The governmenT allowed us To Take only a few of our cloThes, noThing else. We didn'T have any money wiTh us. Our family in The UniTed STaTes had To supporT us unTil my faTher goT seTTled and sTarTed working again. We had To sTarT a whole new life for ourselves.

I know I can never repay my parenTs for geTTing my broTher and me ouT of Cuba so ThaT we could come here To This free counTry and do whaT we please. If iT weren'T for Them, I don'T know where I would be. righT now. I'm jusT Thankful ThaT I have The freedom To Tell abouT Communism in The besT way I can To Those who don'T know how bad iT is.

—Raysa Delgado, 11Th grade

Note: Published in the 1982 *Rain Dance Review* by Baldwin High School. Used with permission.

plaque at the school board meeting, and winners of all ages read their writing from the stage at the mall. In addition, winning papers are published in a special supplement of the local newspaper. The literary contest is a way to truly celebrate writing in a dramatic way.

Letter-Video Exchanges

Another method of publishing is letter-video exchanges between classes in different parts of the country. In a letter-video exchange between reluctant writers in Nancy Krim's class at Scarsdale High School in Scarsdale, New York, and my classes at Baldwin High School in Milledgeville, Georgia, students revealed stereotypes they had formed about one another. Stacy, from Scarsdale, writes how she thinks students from Georgia probably view them:

> They probably think that we are stuck up or snobby, but we are not. They think we are rich. Some people in Scarsdale are wealthy and stuck-up and self-centered, but there are many people in Scarsdale who are nice. We are ordinary people who live in a nice town. We go to school for five days and on weekends spend time with people we know. I realize that these two places are very different, and Scarsdale has wealth, but it doesn't mean everyone is snobby.

Pen Pals

Another way to publish students is to join older students with younger students. One semester my advanced placement students became pen pals with 2nd and 5th grade students. Throughout the year, pen pals on both sides looked forward to receiving letters. The older students tried to be good examples for the younger ones, and the younger students tried to please, told about their lives, and looked up to their older mentors. At the end of the year, the elementary students rode a bus to the high school for a party in the media center. I remember walking around the library that day, watching my students talking and exchanging gifts with their pen pals. The younger students were telling my students stories and showing off the books they had written for the older students; everyone had a present to give.

Interactive Writing

Interactive writing is a way for students to exchange letters with an adult who writes as their equal. Interactive writing may be done between the teacher and the students. In interactive writing, the teacher or adult does not try to become an advisor or to pass judgment, but acts in the capacity as a responder.

Another way to create interactive writing is to create an anonymous responder or letter writer. For example, a large stuffed animal in the corner of the room can be the responder or letter partner to all students. A parent volunteer can play this role and write in the voice of the stuffed animal.

Interactive writing is a great way to motivate children to write. Nigel Hall (1994) writes,

> Interactive writing seems to carry its own hook. The hook is getting replies—genuine, meaningful replies. Receiving a reply is the most powerful motivator possible. It tells . . . [children] that someone has taken very seriously what they have written. Wanting to respond to such an interested audience is one of the most powerful reasons for authorship. (Hall & Robinson, p. 8)

Writing for Younger Children

Students may write stories and books for younger students. Regardless of the grade, there is nearly always somebody younger who would like to read the stories. For example, 3rd graders can write books that 1st graders can use to learn to read. Or, students can create a pamphlet or set of instructions on how to survive the 3rd grade.

Autobiography Brochure

Students can write their life story into a threefold brochure that they create on the computer using a publishing program. Brochure sections are (1) where I have been, (2) where I am now, (3) where I am going, and (4) something creative that I wrote. The students can decorate the front panel; the last panel is left blank for overflowing copy, graphics, or a mailing label.

Class Newsletter

Students may publish work in a class newsletter created with a computer publishing program. Each student types his own section. Final newsletters may be given to hospitals, nursing homes, and doctors' offices.

Oral History or Story Sharing

Students of all ages may interview local senior citizens and publish their stories. My students have published a book that contains 110 stories from local residents as told to students from Baldwin High School. Thanks to a Georgia Humanities Grant, several teachers in other counties in the state have conducted similar story-gathering projects in their home communities.

Publishing Steps on the Wall

A 3rd grade teacher, Medra Hartley, publishes each stage of the writing process on the wall outside her classroom. Walking by her room, you can see all the steps of her students' work—from prewriting to the revision. For example, Figures 5.5 (p. 114) through 5.8 (p. 116) show the steps that her student, Joanna, followed in writing her childhood memory paper. Publishing the stages allows us a peek into the process at work, from prewriting through the helping circle and through revision and proofreading.

Assessment and Evaluation

Teachers tend to avoid teaching writing because there are too many papers to grade. Traditionally, in the teacher-expert model, students turn in the papers and the teacher spends hour after hour marking errors. Grading writing becomes a tedium that can only be described

If something inside you is real, we will probably find it interesting, and it will probably be universal. . . . If you are writing the clearest, truest words you can find and doing the best you can to understand and communicate, this will shine on paper like its own little lighthouse.

—Anne Lamott,
Bird by Bird, p. 226

*When I grew up and
began making [spoon
bread] myself, I discovered that the best part is
the cleanup, when I get
to scrape the sides of the
soufflé dish for the
crunchy part that stuck.*

—Martha Freeman,
Writers in the Kitchen, *p. 4*

Figure 5.5

JOANNA'S PREWRITING EXERCISE

My Childhood Memory

1. The Time I cuT my knee.
2. The Time my kiTTen scared me.
3. The Time I lerned To ride my bike.

Senses in My Story

I felT scared. (I screamed.)
My kiTTen was black.
My kiTTen was quiTe.

**The First Sentence to
My Story:** When I was siTing in
The dark green chair in The
living room, my kiTTen ran in.

—Joanna, 3rd grade

---

as "hunt and shoot." A teacher may give a *C* because "I've been teaching long enough to know a *C* paper when I see one." Well, quite frankly, I never learned to know a *C* paper when I saw one.

We need to create ways to grade writing that make sense to kids and lighten the load on teachers. Try creating a rubric to go along with writing projects. Choose approximately five important qualities for a particular assignment and weight each quality by a percent that is based on its importance to the overall assignment. See Figure 5.9 (p. 117) for a sample rating sheet. Sample score sheets for grading are in Figures 5.10 (p. 118), 5.11 (p. 119), and 5.12 (p. 120). The score sheets break down the aspects of an assignment so that students can understand their grade and use the knowledge

Figure 5.6
JOANNA'S ROUGH DRAFT

The Time My Kitten Scared Me

One afternoon, when I was sitting in the dark green chair in the living room, my kitten ran in. I screamed! My mom and dad came into the living room. I told them "I thought my kitten was a black rat." I started taking deep breaths and saw my kitten named Emily hiding behind the coffee table. Then I got up and went into the kitchen to do my homework. My kitten started to play with a string. I began to think it was kind of silly that I thought my kitten was a black rat.

—Joanna, 3rd grade

Figure 5.7
JOANNA'S HELPING CIRCLE NOTES

What Time?	Age and size of cat?	Home alone?
Scare parents?		Were parents?
What colors?	What time of year?	What day?
Run fast?		What year?
Hide?	Age of me?	How many K's?
Were?	Were was chair?	Wher from?

—Joanna, 3rd grade

Figure 5.8
Joanna's Revision

The Time My Kitten Scared Me

One afternoon when I was sitting in the dark green chair in the living room, my kitten ran in. I screamed! My mom and dad came into the living room. I told them that I thought my kitten was a black rat! I started taking deep breaths and saw my kitten hiding behind the coffee table. Then I got up and went into the kitchen to do my homework. My kittens name is Emily. She started to play with a ball of string. I began to think it was kind of silly that I thought my kitten was a rat.

—Joanna, 3rd grade

> The personality behind the writing is so important. . . . On the paper there are all the neatly written words and sentences. It may be completely objective, with "I" not written there once. But behind the words and sentences, there is this deep, important, moving thing—the personality of the writer.
>
> —Brenda Ueland,
> If You Want to Write, p. 127

to improve. Score sheets offer a less subjective, more accurate way to assign a number grade to a writing assignment than traditional grading, which is often a letter grade based on vague criteria or simply points taken off for each error.

Grading writing using teacher-made rubrics makes justifying writing grades much easier for the teacher, who can easily explain the rationale to administrators, parents, and students. In addition, the rubric can be easily patterned after state-mandated writing test rubrics, therefore helping the teacher to prepare students for external evaluation beyond the classroom.

Score Sheets

To show students that you believe their prewriting steps are as important as their final copies, try creating score sheets that give

Figure 5.9
RATING SHEET FOR WRITING

C&O   Content & Organization

1 (poor)   2 (fair)   3 (good)   4 (excellent)
Your paper had a developed, controlling idea, which was established through relevant, supporting ideas. The manner in which you presented your ideas was logical. Movement from one idea to another was smooth, and your paper was complete.

S   Style

1 (poor)   2 (fair)   3 (good)   4 (excellent)
Your paper demonstrated some individuality. The tone of your paper was acceptable for your topic, reader, and your purpose. Good voice, honesty, and mind pictures.

SF   Sentence Formation

1 (poor)   2 (fair)   3 (good)   4 (excellent)
You did/did not write effective sentences. You need to be more careful about writing complete sentences and in putting sentence elements together properly. Watch out for fragments, run-ons, and comma splices. Be sure to put a period at the end of each sentence.

U   Usage

1 (poor)   2 (fair)   3 (good)   4 (excellent)
Your paper did/did not demonstrate a sufficient grasp of standard American English. Be particularly careful about pronoun reference, subject-verb agreement, and the proper form for nouns and verbs (errors that you can hear).

M   Mechanics

1 (poor)   2 (fair)   3 (good)   4 (excellent)
Your paper had/did not have numerous mechanical errors. Be especially careful about capitalizing, punctuation, spelling, and indenting (errors that you can see).

Total Points _____

Grading Key:

A's	B's	C's	D's
20=100	17=89	14=79	9=69
19=95	16=85	13=77	8=64
18=92	15=82	12=75	7=59
		11=73	6=54
		10=70	5=49

Figure 5.10
SCORE SHEET

Name: ————————————————————

Prewriting: ———— (10 pts.)

Rough Draft: ———— (10 pts.)

Helping Circle Notes: ———— (10 pts.)

Revision: ———— (10 pts.)

Proofreading: ———— (10 pts.)

Final Draft (50%)

    Content & Organization: ———— (10 pts.)

    Style: ———— (10 pts.)

    Sentence Formation: ———— (10 pts.)

    Usage: ———— (10 pts.)

    Mechanics: ———— (10 pts.)

                       TOTAL: ————

50 percent credit for prewriting steps and 50 percent for the final copy, as in Figures 5.10 and 5.11 (p. 119). As students complete each step, give them their credit. I usually staple each completed step to the back of the score sheet to help students see their progress and to reinforce the idea that all parts of the writing process count.

One special perk of this style of teaching is that on the days that students are prewriting, completing their rough draft, having a helping circle, revising, and proofreading, the teacher goes home without any papers to grade. In addition, students receive credit through a simplified grading process that recognizes hard work at each step of the writing process. Although teachers seem to be grading fewer papers, students are learning to write in the best possible way, the way practicing writers work.

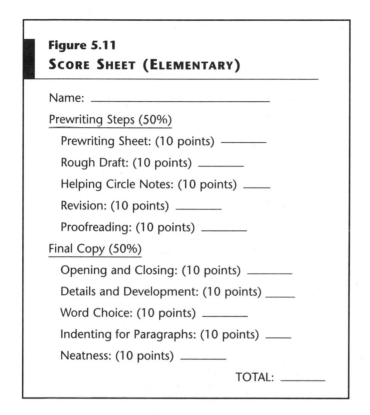

Figure 5.11
SCORE SHEET (ELEMENTARY)

Name: _____

Prewriting Steps (50%)

   Prewriting Sheet: (10 points) _____

   Rough Draft: (10 points) _____

   Helping Circle Notes: (10 points) _____

   Revision: (10 points) _____

   Proofreading: (10 points) _____

Final Copy (50%)

   Opening and Closing: (10 points) _____

   Details and Development: (10 points) _____

   Word Choice: (10 points) _____

   Indenting for Paragraphs: (10 points) _____

   Neatness: (10 points) _____

                       TOTAL: _____

Figure 5.10 (p. 118) is a sample score sheet that I often use. Figure 5.11 is a sheet an elementary teacher created when I asked her to select criteria for a particular assignment. Figure 5.12 (p. 120) is a score sheet for the house story activity.

Writing Notebook Evaluations

Weekly notebooks, like freewrites, can simply be assigned points and students earn a completion grade for accomplishing the assignment. Notebooks, like freewriting, benefit students and are not for evaluating or grading. To ensure that students keep their work, tell them that you will check their notebook periodically. Your review should be for completion only; the grade can be similar to the freewrites (a weekly grade). Don't let students dispose of the writing

Figure 5.12
SCORE SHEET FOR HOUSE STORY

Name: _____

Preliminary Steps (50%)

Prewriting Sheet (10 points): _____

Rough Draft ("Sloppy Copy") (10 points): _____

Helping Circle Notes (10 points) : _____

Revision (10 points): _____

Proofreading (10 points): _____

   Signatures: _____

                _____

                _____

Final Draft (50%)

   Capitalization (10 points): _____

   Punctuation (10 points): _____

   Sentence Formation (10 points): _____

   Content (10 points): _____

   Organization (10 points): _____

                         TOTAL: _____

they have done. They will use these writing notebooks again and again to observe their progress, to get ideas for future writing, and to build confidence in their writing ability. Their growing notebook is a source of pride as well as a rich resource for future writing ideas.

Summary

Publishing increases an author's pride in her work. Through publishing, the writing done in the classroom can be one of those memories a student can cherish for years. The teacher, in fact, may become part of a student's favorite memories. Grading papers can truly become what we all believe it should be—a way to help students learn.

Suggestions for the Teacher

◆ Publish your work when you publish student work.

◆ Share the writing between your class and a class in another grade level, school, city, state, or country. Don't overlook the Internet as a possibility.

◆ Use publishing to let the school—better yet, the whole community—know about the writing that is taking place in your classroom.

Tea Cakes

1 cup shortening, room temperature

2 1/2 cups sugar

4 beaten eggs

4 cups self-rising flour

1 1/2 teaspoons vanilla

finely chopped nuts or colored candies for topping (optional)

◆ Cream the shortening and sugar. Gradually add beaten eggs, flour, and vanilla, mixing well. Knead a few times on a floured surface until the dough is easy to work with. Roll out the dough until paper thin. (As you fold, shape, and roll the dough, the flour on your surface will get mixed in. Add flour to the rolling pin, your hands, and the dough as you work.) Cut the dough with cookie cutters into shapes; sprinkle with nuts or colored candies if desired.

◆ Place an inch apart on a lightly greased cookie sheet and bake at 350° for 10–12 minutes. If the tea cakes are small, baking may take less time. Tea cakes are ready when they are still white, with only slight browning around the edges. Take them off the cookie sheet with a spatula, and allow to cool thoroughly on a wire rack. Makes about 3 dozen crispy tea cakes. Store in an airtight container.

Creating Poetry and Having Fun with Writing

6

As a child, I stood in the kitchen and watched as Mama covered the countertop with a soft white cloth. The flour and sugar she kept in drawers under the counter, and I watched her hand disappear into the drawer and emerge to sprinkle the flour onto the white cloth and roll out the sweet white cookie dough with the wooden rolling pin. Using aluminum cookie cutters with scalloped edges, she cut into thin flat rounds of dough, lifted the soft shapes, and placed them on the cookie sheet, leaving the leftover edges of dough on the white cloth. These leftover dough edges she made into a ball, then rolled out again, and cut again until the pieces left were too small for a whole cookie. Those last little pieces were mine to peel up off the flour and put into my mouth. I can still taste the soft white sweetness.

I also spent a lot of time in the kitchen of my mother's older sister, Nannie Prosser, who lived across town. It was always a special day when we arrived at her house, and the kitchen was filled with that familiar smell of tea cakes. Somehow, although my grandmothers died before I was born and I didn't know where grandmothers came from, I must have associated baking and the idea of grandmothers. So one day as my aunt was making tea cakes in her kitchen, I blurted out, "How about you being my Granny?" She agreed, and from that day forward, Granny became the person, other than Mama, who made tea cakes for us. Granny was older than Mama; the tea cake recipe probably came from her. All I know is that those cookies were a symbol that all was right with the world, and, at either house, we were special and loved.

Writers perform rituals. They stack books, they sharpen pencils, they arrange and rearrange their workspace to get it exactly the way they want it. When writing poetry, they move words around, lengthen and shorten lines, and grab little images that pass through their minds. Like sprinkling colored sugar and rolling and rearranging dough, they assemble and create and add the final touches. And they use their childhood memories with all the associated senses, those like touching soft, floured dough and breathing in the wonderful smell that comes with baking cookies. Handling delicate sheets of thin dough takes practice, like handling words—a reminder that we learn to cook by cooking and we learn to write by writing.

Poetry

Poetry is a powerful tool in any writing program. The condensed form of poetry enables us to teach imagery (or mind pictures), forms and patterns, voice, honesty, and many of the characteristics of writing that we also teach through prose. Dan Kirby and Tom Liner (1988) write in *Inside Out,*

> In poetry, as in all writing, the technical aspects of the poem are really of secondary importance; good writing is <u>honest</u> writing. The writer risks feelings with us, and we respond to the words because they touch our feelings through shared human experiences. (p. 74)

Poetry comes naturally to children. Many of the activities in this book can be done in the form of poetry, but I have a few favorite poetry activities that I will include here. Please don't save poetry and other fun writing activities until Fridays or to the end to a course or year. As Lucy Calkins (1994) writes in *The Art of Teaching Writing,* " 'Poetry,' Eudora Welty has said, 'is the school I went to in order to learn to write prose.' Poetry can also be the school our children go

---

"Can I write a poem instead?". . .

I stalled him. "Look, what about one of those other writings? How about an interview with one of the characters in the story?" Was he trying to duck the assignment? He hadn't done much so far with his writing.

"Naw," he said, "I got an idea, but it's a poem. I don't feel like doing none of that other stuff." So much for planning. But he did look as if he was interested.

"Do it," I said. He smiled and went back to his seat in the back of the room.

—Kirby and Liner,
Inside Out, *pp. 72–73*

to in order to write prose" (p. 370). Sprinkle poetry liberally through-out your writing program and consider how it helps students learn to use language, to write imagery, to practice form, and to express their feelings through writing.

The Imitation Poem

The imitation poem is a great way to let children see the beauty of the language of poetry and the way words flow together to make sounds and images. Give students a copy of a poem written by a famous poet, and read the poem aloud. Point out to them the way the poem is composed of sentences, and show them how to find the parts of speech, including the nouns, verbs, and adjectives.

Ask students to imitate the poem, word-by-word, line-by-line. Where there is a noun, they will put a noun; where there is a verb, they should write a verb; where there is an adjective, they write an adjective. Margaret Walker's "Memory"(1989) is a good poem for introducing this activity. I also love to use the poetry of William Carlos Williams. Figure 6.1 is student Jack Peckham's imitation poem of Williams's "The Red Wheelbarrow" (1951).

I formed the habit long ago of putting new poems into a desk drawer and letting them lie there to ripen (or the opposite) like apples.

—Archibald MacLeish,
In Writers at Work: The Paris Review Interviews, p. 130

Figure 6.1
Imitation Poem on Baseball

So Much Depends
So much depends
Upon
A hard round
Ball
Flying aT my glove
Only
Inches away from OuT Three?
                    —3rd grade

And what great writers
actually pass on is not
so much their words,
but they hand on their
breath at their moments
of inspiration. If you
read a great poem
aloud—for example,
'To a Skylark' by Percy
Bysshe Shelley—and
read it the way he set it
up and punctuated it,
what you are doing is
breathing his inspired
breath at the moment
he wrote that poem.
That breath was so
powerful it still can be
awakened in us over
150 years later. Taking it
on is very exhilarating.
This is why it is good to
remember: if you want
to get high, don't drink
whiskey; read Shake-
speare, Tennyson, Keats,
Neruda, Hopkins, Millay,
Whitman, aloud and let
your body sing.

—Natalie Goldberg,
Writing Down the Bones,
p. 51

Figure 6.2
IMITATION POEM ON A CAR

> This Is Just To Say
>
> I have wrecked
> Your $45,000 car
> That you keep
> Parked in The garage
> And which
> You probably
> Polish
> Every weekend
>
> Forgive me
> That's just
> The way The Mercedes
> Benz
>   —Bill Allen, 11Th grade

Source: Published in the 1985 *Rain Dance Review* by Baldwin High School. Used with permission.

Another poem by William Carlos Williams, "This is Just to Say" (1951, p. 354), is wonderful for inspiring students to write about something they have to say that they're sorry for, but they aren't *really* sorry for. See Figure 6.2 for a student's imitation poem using "This is Just to Say" as a base.

Oral Poetry Readings

This activity is wonderful for helping students to appreciate the sound of poetry. Ask the media specialist to fill a rolling cart with anthologies of poetry, enough for each student to have a book.

Students then prepare to give readings of their favorite poems from the podium in front of the room. Students practice by reading aloud to one another, and they learn that reading poetry isn't like reading prose; to read poetry, they need to make eye contact, stand on both feet, and read very, very slowly with meaning—the way practicing poets give readings, pausing at all the poignant moments. Students who need lots of personal attention especially enjoy this activity. The students quickly learn to love poetry, and reading poems aloud improves their writing and reading as well as their confidence.

Poetry readings are a wonderful way for us to help our students appreciate the beauty of language. Wherever possible, enable your students to attend poetry readings. You can invite neighborhood poets into the classroom, and you can arrange field trips for younger students or bribe older students to attend local poetry events by trading a vocabulary test or some other task for their attendance. After all, what are a few new vocabulary words, some of which they probably already know anyway, when compared with a chance to appreciate the beauty of words in poetry?

Putting Unlikes Together

A teacher at a workshop once told me that she and her daughter often play a game of putting unlikes together and making up poetry and stories about them. When walking through the woods, for example, one of them will say, "an old soda can and a tree stump." The other will begin, "The old man sat his soda down on the stump and looked up into the sky." To build on this idea, create a box of odd things (a shoe, pencil sharpener, chalk, baseball), and a box of ideas or qualities (honesty, courage, beauty, truth, love) written on little slips of paper. Have students draw one item and one idea or quality from each box and make up a poem.

Imagination Poem

Writing an imagination poem encourages students to be very creative. The object is to write a poem about what is inside a cloud or a tree trunk or what is under the ground or above the sky.

Suggest that students go to such a place in their imagination and write a poem from that place.

Poetry from Honest Feelings and Childhood Memories

There are three steps to writing poetry from honesty and memories. The first two will get the ideas flowing.

1. Have students think of a childhood memory that is connected with strong feelings and do a free write about the predominant feeling (anger, sadness, happiness, guilt, fear). Tell students to think about how the feeling *looked* on them. To help the students get started, share some of your own childhood feelings.

2. Have students talk about these memories and these feelings in classroom circles.

3. Then have students choose one line from their freewriting that can be a first line for a poem. Have them write this line at the top of a page, and see where it goes from there.

Figures 6.3 through 6.5 show several student samples.

Poetry is powerful because of the ways it can enrich people's lived lives. Poems can be read aloud at Thanksgiving dinner or at a baby's baptism. Poems can be put onto greeting cards or framed and given as gifts. Poems can also be woven into the life of a classroom community—posted next to the aquarium, chanted as a ritualized opening to every day's math class, hung on the classroom door as a motto for the community.

—Lucy Calkins,
The Art of Teaching Writing,
p. 371

Figure 6.3
HONEST FEELINGS POEM

Scared

Scared is a bad feeling To have
Scared is when IT lighTnings and Thunders
Scared is when you see a ghosT
Scared is when you geT in Trouble
and everybody finds you ouT.
Scared is when your parenTs geT a divorce,
And IT mighT be your faulT.

—6Th grade

Figure 6.4
FEELINGS POEM WRITING

Daddy

Daddy, ever since you left me,
My life hasn't been The same.
When you don't come see me,
I really feel ashamed.

Is iT me why you left?

—9Th grade

Figure 6.5
CHILDHOOD MEMORY POEM

Feelings Poem

Two years ago,
My grandmoTher died.
I was very sad.
I wenT To her grave.
When I Think abouT iT,
I feel very sad.
I wish my grandmoTher
would noT die.

—Mac Babb, 5Th grade

Poetry for Special Gifts

For special occasions, have students write poems to give as gifts. They can buy an inexpensive frame and type their poems in a pretty font and decorate them on the computer. What present could mean more on Mother's Day? A 9th grader wrote the poem in Figure 6.6 (p. 130) for her mother on Valentine's Day.

The Shape of Poetry in Everyday Life

Help students see the poetry in their everyday lives. They can write poetry about breakfast cereal, sneakers, the girl who sits in front of them in class, the school lunchroom, or a pencil. See Figure 6.7 (p. 131) for a wonderful sample.

Other Fun Writing Activities

Sprinkle pleasant writing activities throughout the school year. Some may be very brief, just five minutes at the beginning of class.

Many years ago, when I
was teaching one of my
first English courses, I
came across Ask Your
Mama, a collection of
poems by Langston
Hughes. In one, the
recurring image, 'in a
leaf of collard, green,'
came back to haunt me.
I, too, have been
marked by the large,
purplish-tinged leaves
that are, along with
okra and watermelon,
the African Americans'
culinary mark of Cain.
Collard greens have
followed me all of my life
and remain something
I don't want to live
without. They have
punctuated my life per-
fuming each phase with
their pungent aroma.

—Jessica B. Harris,

"In a Leaf of Collard, Green,"
We Are What We Ate, p. 105

Figure 6.6
GIFT POEM

Mama

I come To school each and every day
Because Mama said iT had To be ThaT way.
I respecT Those who respecT me
Because ThaT's whaT Mama expecTs of me
She is a person ThaT I can TrusT
She doesn'T expecT someone else To babysiT us.
We're big enough To keep ourselves
By sTaying ouT of Trouble and noT going To jail.
I would risk my life for my moTher
And help her if There's a pain she suffers.
We acT like young ladies are supposed To acT
Because if we don'T Mama will say I didn'T
Raise you To be a braT.
I'm gonna be all I can possibly be
Because a career is whaT Mama sees in me.
                              —9Th grade girl

Others may stretch through several days, or class periods, using the
writing process to create finished pieces.

Orange Activity

This is a great activity for the last day before winter vacation or
the end of the school year. Give each student an orange, and tell
the students to write a detailed description of their oranges. They

---

Figure 6.7
EVERYDAY SHAPES POEM

Cheerios

They float like little lifesavers in a white lake.
They bump together or float alone.
I can spear them on my fork
Or bounce them up and down with my spoon.
Then, in the end, I eat them.
—Allie Johns, 6th grade

---

should notice color, shape, and size as related to the others in the room, as well as smoothness of the peel and any special markings. Next, collect all the oranges and line them up on a table. Students then come to the front one at a time, identify their own orange, and read their descriptions. Then students get to eat their oranges. You probably won't believe it until you try it, but this works with anything made in nature. I have done this activity successfully with peanuts and 30 teachers as well as with apples, plums, walnuts, and rocks. Alternatively, lemons are great for this activity. After all of the descriptions are read, students peel the lemons and discover that, inside, all the lemons look alike (just like people).

David, an elementary teacher, gave his students popped popcorn. He was amazed at the creative descriptions his students wrote, describing their popcorn pieces as a crab or a rabbit with three ears. As students write these descriptions, they tend to become attached to the object they are describing. Try capitalizing on these feelings of ownership by having students name the orange (peanut, rock, or whatever), tell its hobbies, and explain, "If this [piece of popcorn] were a [teacher, student, parent], what kind would it be?" A sample popcorn biography appears in Figure 6.8 (p. 132).

Figure 6.8
MY POPCORN

My popcorn's name is BoBo. He lives in a bag. His hobby is being eaten. He has wings like elbows and a bump on his head like a wart. He is so ugly he doesn't have any friends. So I will just put him out of his misery and eat him. The End of BoBo.
                                                                    —2nd grade

---

Thank You, Ma'am

Read aloud to students Langston Hughes's "Thank You, Ma'am" (1996), a story in which a young boy tries to steal from an elderly woman and is, instead, taught a lesson. Ask students to write a story about an older friend or relative who has been nice to them or who is special to them for some reason. Or, ask them to write about a time they took something that wasn't theirs.

Letter to a Child

Ask your students to imagine that one day each one of them will be a parent. With that thought in mind, each student should write a letter to that future child. In writing this letter, the author should tell the child about his hopes and fears. In addition, students should address some of the choices this child will have and offer some advice, such as how can the child stay on the right track in life? What can the child expect from the student as a parent?

Letter to Yourself

Have each student write a letter to himself. The letter is to be saved and opened when the student is 80 years old—or any age older than now. Include aspirations and dreams—what does the student hope to accomplish by 80 years old? For a different, more immediate twist on this assignment, ask each student to write a letter on the first day of school, with the understanding that the letters will be saved and read at the end of the semester or year.

Letter to a Person with Magical Powers

Have students write letters to a person with magical powers and ask that person to change something in the students' lives or to add something to their lives that will make a difference to them. Have them include in the letter how the change will affect their lives.

Group Story

Divide the class into groups with four or five students. Give each group a sheet of paper with one sentence on it. Each student, in turn, must write the next sentence on the paper to help form a story. When the last student receives the paper, it is returned to the first student. That student has a second chance to add a sentence to the story and to see how the story has progressed. After everyone has finished, the students can polish their story together by adding or deleting sentences. After they are satisfied with their story, they can select a leader from the group to read the story aloud to the class. The following sentences can help get this assignment started: (1) There were muddy footprints around the outside of the school. (2) Jessica knew she was in trouble, and she knew that she must do something soon. (3) The small, torn piece of paper said to meet them at the secret hideout after school. (4) The office aide told Alex to report to the principal's office immediately.

Group Directions

Divide the class into groups of about four students each. Have each group agree on a place in town, and then write directions from the school to that place (without naming the destination). The directions should be so thorough that someone unfamiliar with the area could find the place. Then have groups exchange papers and try to identify the place by following the directions in their minds.

Our family spends many hours working together—planting and harvesting and running the farm stand where we sell peaches, okra, crowder peas, and all the other wonderful produce we grow. Often when we're working we find ourselves talking about the past, and what we seem to remember most is the food.

—Dori Sanders,
Dori Sanders' Country Cooking, pp. IX–XV

Having students work in groups to formulate these directions promotes interaction and is an activity that often helps students see that what they write isn't always exactly what they thought or meant to write (e.g., they may leave out a key street). Instead of directions to a location, the groups could write directions for performing a task or making something, such as programming a VCR, oiling a lawn mower, servicing a car, or baking a cake.

Childhood Map

For this exercise, students draw a map of their room, a map of their neighborhood, or perhaps a map of their kitchen. Then have them imagine and describe a scene in the place they mapped. An alternative would be to pretend to look in the windows of a childhood home to see the people. Then have students freewrite about their experience. Your may give students an assignment like this one:

> You are standing outside the home you lived in as a child. Look at the outside of the house. Look at the material it is made of. Step up to the window. Look inside. You see people in there. Look closely to see what they are doing. Now, describe what you see.

A student's response is in Figure 6.9 (p. 135).

Thank-You Notes

One of my mother's pet peeves was receiving thank-you notes that didn't say anything, such as "Thank you for the gift. I'm sure it will come in handy." She felt that writing thank-you notes was becoming a lost art. Mama would put a lot of thought and work into finding a gift that she thought the recipient would want, and would be peeved when the thank-you note didn't even mention the gift.

There are many good reasons to add thank-you notes to school writing programs. Students need to know how to write personal, honest, specific notes with a real audience. In the real world of

The professional writer may write for himself, but he does not write to himself. The writer does not exist without a reader. The purpose of writing is not to arrange ink on paper, to provide a mirror for the author's thoughts, but to carry ideas and information from the mind of one person into the mind of another.

—Donald M. Murray,
A Writer Teaches Writing,
p. 3

Figure 6.9
MY CHILDHOOD WINDOW

I am looking in my window where my room used To be. My mama is in There making up my bed. I can see her puT my favoriTe Teddy bear in The middle. Then my daddy comes in and calls ouT, "Where is Ana? I canT find her." I knock on The window and he looks up and I wave. He was glad To find me.

—Anise Veal, 4Th grade

school, they will be expected to write thank-you notes for graduation gifts as well as for letters of reference written by teachers. Thank-you notes are good writing activities because they are brief and are an excellent showcase for what students have learned about good writing. Their thank-you notes should be personal, honest, in their real voice, and specific to the gift itself.

Newspaper Stories

Many published writers say they use newspapers to spark ideas for writing. Students can also use newspaper headlines as inspiration. From newspaper articles we find characters, funny plots, and the many absurdities of the human condition. Suggest that students make up the story that could go behind the headline.

Some of my favorite headlines are "Two Fall to Death in Dodging Kiss," "He Criticized Gift, So She Shot Him," and "Wedding Pictures and Dead Groom Found in Storage Unit."

Games

Classroom sets of some board games will get students talking together in groups, and, from these conversations, many good writing topics will surface. Explore the aisle of board games in your local stores for those that promote "tale telling."

Summary

Many published writers describe writing as fun and involving play. When teaching students, we also must have ideas that are creative and that allow choice and enough time to give room for play and experimentation with words and ideas. In addition, when students study the writing of published writers, they can see the play written between the lines.

Unfortunately, not all writing in school seems like play. The ideas in Chapter 7 can help students learn to do the kind of writing they need to succeed in school-writing situations—while learning how to approach writing like professional writers. And, as you will see, even school writing can be creative and fun.

Suggestions for the Teacher

◆ Craft your own imitation poems to share with students.

◆ Collect funny newspaper headlines to use for writing ideas and ask students to be on the lookout, too.

◆ Create a story that takes place in your childhood room, your neighborhood, or a secret place. Share your story with your students.

Evelyn opened her purse and gave Mrs. Thread-goode one of the pimiento-cheese sand-wiches she had wrapped in wax paper, and brought from home. Mrs. Threadgoode was delighted. "Oh, thank you! I love a good pimiento-cheese sandwich. In fact, I love anything to eat that's a pretty color."

—Fannie Flagg,
Fried Green Tomatoes at the Whistle Stop Café, p. 47

Mama's Lemon Cake

Ingredients for the cake:

1 package white cake mix	2/3 cup cooking oil
1 small package lemon Jello gelatin	2/3 cup water
4 eggs	1 teaspoon lemon flavoring

Ingredients for the orange glaze:

1 cup sugar	1/2 teaspoon salt
1 cup orange juice	1 1/2 teaspoons lemon juice
4 tablespoons cornstarch	2 teaspoons butter

◆ Preheat the oven to 350°. Use a spoon to mix the dry gelatin with the cake mix. Beat in the eggs, one at a time, by hand or with a mixer. Then add cooking oil, water, and lemon flavoring. Beat well. Pour the mixture into a greased and floured medium-sized tube pan. Cook until golden brown, about 1 hour. Turn the cake onto a cooling rack and let cool completely before glazing.

◆ To make the glaze, mix all of the ingredients together in a saucepan. Bring to a rolling boil and boil 1 minute, stirring constantly. Chill the glaze until the consistency is stiff or like store-bought icing, then glaze the cake.

Making School Writing Real

7

MY FATHER, HARVEY WORSHAM, WAS MY MOTHER'S SWEETHEART, AND SHE NEVER stopped missing him after his death. Sunday afternoons seemed to be her lonely times. It was at those times that she went into the kitchen, baked her lemon cake, and took it to someone.

As I grew older and began to be interested in Mama's recipes, I started asking her how to make certain dishes and why she didn't write down her recipes. She always answered that it was too complicated to try to remember and write it all down. She said I could just come over and watch her sometime. So that's what I did. I brought a notebook and a pen, and I sat on a little pink stool in the corner of her kitchen, writing down the steps as she baked.

This chapter involves the kind of writing most akin to my sitting on a little pink stool in my mother's kitchen, writing down the steps to follow in a recipe. All over the United States school districts are emphasizing testing. Teachers are forced to spend class time getting students ready for tests because of an increasing emphasis on raising standards and finding ways to measure success. Getting ready often involves learning and practicing the steps to follow, some very restrictive.

There are several ways we can respond to this phenomenon. We can gripe and whine and complain. We can feel sorry for ourselves. Or we can follow the example of my Mama and her lemon cake, pick ourselves up, and carry on. Carrying on means that we

> [My Mother's] special genre [for writing] is the recipe. For most, a recipe is a straightforward exercise in giving directions: a list of ingredients, step-by-step instructions, perhaps a few serving suggestions. But for my mother, a recipe represents an opportunity to experiment with composing as well as cooking. Her recipes are exercises in narration, description, analysis, even argument. . . . They are nothing like Betty Crocker ever imagined."
>
> —Sharon L. Jansen, "Family Liked 1956: My Mother's Recipes," Through the Kitchen Window, p. 55

must acknowledge that testing is not going away. We cannot, however, let testing cause us to focus only on those things that will be tested, at the expense of other important parts of a student's development as a human being. We need ways to help students become well-rounded writers, not just writers who follow directions at the expense of creativity and experimentation in writing, ignoring the way successful writers write.

School Writing and Real Writing

I believe that there are two kinds of writing: "school" writing and "real" writing. School writing is writing that (1) is used for testing purposes, (2) has to be completed within a certain time period, (3) is written on an assigned topic which the writer may or may not know or care anything about, and (4) should be as perfect as possible the first time, with very little chance for revision. School writing does not mirror the writing authors do in the real world.

Real writing, on the other hand, is written the way published writers write: (1) the writer may choose a topic about which she feels knowledgeable, a topic that *matters*; (2) the writer may take time to let her ideas develop naturally; and (3) the writer may revise as many times as necessary to get it right. Real writing is written for real reasons—to communicate, to entertain, to enlighten, and to inform.

Yet, real or not, school writing is still a fact of school life. And the need to succeed in school is very real to teachers, students, administrators, and parents. It was real when we were in school, and it is real to our students now.

If, because we do not believe that school writing should be something separate from real writing, we refuse to teach our students how to handle school writing, then we are denying them success in their school writing experiences. We *must* teach school writing, as well as real writing, to our students—and, yes, sometimes we must teach formulas. If a formula will be useful to our students in school, then we must teach it to them.

Making School Writing Real

Real writing is good writing. It contains that uniqueness of the writer's personality that is all too often omitted from the formulaic versions of school writing. To transform school writing into real writing, we need to create ways of bringing those elements of the real to the artificial. Following are some methods for making school writing real.

Follow the real writing process. When teaching school writing, be sure to take students through the various stages of the process that real writers use. Have students prewrite, conduct helping circles, revise, and proofread; then publish their work. In the same way a newspaper reporter must meet a deadline, help students learn to write according to a time limit for those school-writing situations where a limit is necessary or required.

Teach students to develop middle paragraphs by using real, personal details to support main points. All writing should be *interesting*, whether it is school writing or real writing. Despite the need to follow directions or to write using a formula, help students learn to organize their ideas about a topic while including the elements of good writing that real writers use: (1) appealing to the senses—especially taste, smell, and texture; (2) making use of their own locale and sense of place; (3) using their own memories and stories; and (4) expanding and changing the way they follow directions to make their writing better.

Perform the assignments students are asked to write. As teachers, we learn more about how to teach writing by writing along with students, meeting the same time constraints, and writing on the same topics. I remember the first time I tried writing with my advanced placement class. As part of the required curriculum, these students had to write responses to long passages in about 25 minutes. One day I decided to sit down and try to write the paper with them. I set the clock, and we all began to write. When the timer chimed, I had just begun to figure out what I wanted to write. I

This is not my recipe. This is a memory, retrievable only as memories are, by evocation and gesture and occasional concreteness that is not factual. And I resist making it a recipe. This is about art and love, not about technique.

—Elizabeth Kamarck Minnich, "But Really, There Are No Recipes," Through the Kitchen Window, p. 135

stopped, looked up at my class, and said, "Wow! How do you do it?" And together, we figured it out. Students who had been successful in completing the assignment explained to us how they did it. Some made a quick list of all their thoughts on the topic; others did short freewriting; others closed their eyes and visualized the paper they were going to write. Much of learning to write with a deadline is trying different methods until the individual learns what works best.

Try teaching a mixture of real writing and school writing. When practicable, teach students to write a structured essay in various time limits and on assigned topics that may occur in school situations. Students should still follow the writing process, however, and help each other improve through helping circles and proofreading groups. And because the teacher is not the only audience, school writing becomes more real. You will, of course, not always be able to include all steps of the writing process when teaching timed writing. I suggest following all steps, including the helping circle, with one or two school writing assignments. Then, leave out the helping circle, give timed writing assignments, and help them practice with shortened versions of prewriting, rough drafts, proofreading, and final drafts.

School Writing Formulas

When teaching school writing, we often rely on formulas for writing. Two of these are the hamburger paragraph and the five-paragraph theme formula (see p. 12). Formulas give students a predetermined outline, or template, into which they can plug their own ideas and information. Having a formula means having a tool students can use for planning and organizing a paper in a given length of time for testing and other school-writing situations. The writing assignments that follow are based primarily on the five-paragraph format, which is the formula most often used in school. Specifically, the five-paragraph theme formula teaches students to create a thesis statement, which states their opinion on a subject and includes three ideas to develop; to write an introductory paragraph that ends with the thesis statement and a concluding paragraph

But as I sorted through my mother's recipes, really noticing them for the first time, I realized that they were more than ingredients and directions. They were the rich and varied compositions of a writer who had chosen her own form and then pushed beyond the usual limits defining that form.

—*Sharon L. Jansen,*
"Family Liked 1956: My Mother's Recipes," Through the Kitchen Window, *p. 63*

that begins with a restatement of the thesis; and to include transitions that connect the three middle paragraphs to one another. Each middle paragraph develops one of the three main ideas from the thesis statement. Naturally, this is only one formula, but it is representative of other formulas.

Prewriting Sheets: Good Things About Me

In writing for school, students are usually given assigned topics. To get them started, give students prewriting sheets to fill out for various topics. When they are initially learning how to do formula writing, be sure to give them encouraging, upbeat topics that are interesting enough to them to ensure success. For example, give them a personal topic rather than asking their opinion about a political situation or a topic that is too sophisticated for them to easily grasp.

A good topic to use early in trying this writing strategy is "good things about me," a confidence-building topic. Model this task for students by filling out a prewriting sheet and writing a sample paper yourself. Figure 7.1 (p. 144) demonstrates the prewriting sheet. Sharing your writing with students is a wonderful experience and helps to build a trusting atmosphere for writing.

For example, when I fill out my prewriting sheet, I list three good things about me: I am good to my dog, Annie; I was good to my mother; I am a good friend. Then I list my details under each "good thing" (I buy Annie's favorite food and give her treats), and then write my rough draft. I show my prewriting sheet and rough draft to students and indicate where the lists and examples from the prewriting sheet fit into the essay. When teachers write with students, students see that writing is important; the practice also helps teachers learn better how to do it and how to teach it.

One of my reluctant 9th grade writers, Tony James, refused to do this activity when it was first assigned. He sat in front of the blank sheet of paper for a long time. Finally, he began to fill out the prewriting sheet, but when I went to see what he was doing, I saw that he had listed negative things. After much persuasion, I convinced

Figure 7.1
Prewriting Worksheet

Name: _____ Class Period: _____ Date: _____

Topic: Good Things About Me

Prewriting

I.   Write your topic here:

_____

II. Change your topic into one sentence that will be your thesis statement. (This sentence will be the last sentence of your first paragraph and the first sentence of your last paragraph.)

Write your thesis statement here. _____

_____

III. Fill out the following plan by thinking of your three main points and then listing details under each one.

    1. _____

       _____

       _____

    2. _____

       _____

       _____

    3. _____

       _____

       _____

IV. Use one of these ideas for your introduction.
     Tell a little story.
     Give a list of facts.
     Ask a question and answer it.
     Talk in general about the subject.

Choose the idea you would like to use for your introduction and write your introduction here.

_____

_____

Tony to use his negative thoughts for an introduction. As you will see from his paper in Figure 7.2 (p. 146), Tony found that he did have many good things about him. An example of a 4th grade "good things about me" paper is in Figure 7.3 (p. 147).

Sometimes when students have difficulty thinking of good things about them, try letting their classmates help them. There are no better compliments than those that come from a peer group. Figure 7.4 (p. 148) shows an example of a paper that grew from good things listed by classmates.

Some teachers use the list of interesting and unusual things about me from the spotlighting activity in Chapter 2 (see p. 31). Students often keep these sheets in their notebooks—they can look back and circle the facts they would like to use for their paper.

Letter to a Favorite Teacher

One of my favorite activities for school writing is to ask students to write a letter to a favorite teacher. Part of the assignment is for the student to jog the teacher's memory about the student and to mention specific activities and incidents the student remembers from that classroom. After students have worked hard to get these just right, mail the letters to the teacher and send copies to the teacher's principal and the school superintendent for the teacher's file. Teachers usually respond to the letters, so the school-writing activity becomes a real form of communication. The prewriting sheet for this activity is in Figure 7.5 (p. 149). Two 3rd grade samples of this activity are shown in Figures 7.6 (p. 150) and 7.7 (p. 151).

Family History Story

The family history story activity gives students a chance to talk to their parents or older family members or neighbors and to learn about the way things used to be. Students learn what things cost when their family members were the students' age and how their grandparents washed clothes and cooked food. They learn about their own history and how hard their ancestors fought to overcome

Like most farm-family cooks, I don't measure or fuss too much with details. How much of an ingredient? Enough for one good mess, a couple of handfuls or so. What size pan? Whatever I have handy. If it's too small, I just cut down on the amount I'm going to cook. If it's too big, I end up with something cooked for tomorrow as well.

—*Dori Sanders,*
Dori Sanders' Country Cooking, *p. XIV*

Figure 7.2
GOOD THINGS ABOUT ME

Hi! My name is Tony, and I have lots of bad Things about me. For example, I'm always Trying To do Things I shouldn't, like making people feel down on Themselves by always Trying To pick. I also don't do as well in my classes as I could, but There are several good Things about me.

The first good Thing about me is That I love To help my mom around The house. When we have a great big dinner and she doesn't feel Too good, I always wash The dishes for her. I also clean house for my mom. She likes it when I clean The house because she says I leave a special shine To it.

Second of all, I Try To Take Time out from what I'm doing To help others. The Time my sister was pregnant and she needed someone To watch over her house, I was right There for her when she really needed me. Also when my grandmother was sick, I Took Time out To nurse her back To health. I also Take Time out To help The students at my school by Trying To encourage Them To finish school and not To drop out, and I also Tell The kids of my community To stay away from drugs and "Just say no!"

Finally, I'm very kind To all people. I never get mad at anyone, and I also respect my elders. I never Talk back To Them. Mainly I never get into fights with anyone because I'm here To help, not To hurt.

As you can see, There are several Things I Think are excellent about me and also There are several bad Things about me, but I'm going To put That aside and focus on The good Things.

                                        —Tony James, 9Th grade

Note: Published in the 1993 *Rain Dance Review* by Baldwin High School. Used with permission.

Figure 7.3
SAMPLE GOOD THINGS ABOUT ME PAPER

Some people are good, and some are bad. I am a nice person, and There are a loT of good Things abouT me.

The firsT good Thing abouT me is ThaT I am nice To my liTTle broTher. He geTs on my nerves someTimes by geTTing in my sTuff, buT I am usually nice To him excepT someTimes.

The nexT god Thing abouT me is ThaT I do my chores. I clean up my room and help wiTh The dishes, and on SaTurday, I Take ouT The Trash.

The lasT good Thing abouT me is ThaT I am smarT. I always do my homework, and I make good grades in school. I made The highesT grade in The class on our lasT maTh TesT.

As you can see, There are several good Things abouT me. ThaT is why I am proud of myself, and my Mama and Daddy are proud of me Too.

—Kim, 4Th grade

injustices. And they learn how to put this collection of new knowledge together in a well-organized research essay. The family history story is a formula with freedom. And, as a bonus, when younger people mingle with older people and share stories, students are also learning character education. The prewriting sheet for the family history story is in Figure 7.8 (p. 152).

Class Essay: A Teaching Tool for All Subjects

One of my favorite ways to teach school writing is the class essay because it teaches students how to organize formulaic essays in a

---

Figure 7.4
TYRE'S GOOD THINGS ABOUT ME PAPER

I have some good Things about me That I did not know, because I pick on people and all That. But In This story you will find out That I do good Things Too.

One Thing That my friends Told me was That I play football pretty good. That is what I want To play when I grow up. I have been called by The coach To play for B Team.

The second Thing That my friends Told me was That I am nice. Most of The Time I am unless I get in Trouble from a Teacher for nothing. But usually I am nice To everybody because I will help Them and Talk To Them.

And The last Thing That some people Tell me is That my eyes are pretty. Almost everyone ever since I was little would Tell me That my eyes were pretty and all That.

So you see by now That I have some good Things about me and some I did not know until my friends Told me.

—Tyre Conner, 3rd grade

---

way that is effective and fun. The class essay can be used to teach students how to write formula essays for school and may be used for teaching specific content in *any* subject area. It is great for teaching students how to organize information; how to give specific support to main ideas; how to write transitions, introductions, and conclusions; how to structure paragraphs and sentences; and how to work with usage, audience, voice, purpose, editing, proofreading, and

Figure 7.5
PREWRITING WORKSHEET

Topic: My Favorite Teacher _____

Thesis statement: There are several reasons why you were my favorite teacher. _____

First main idea: _____

      Details to support the first main idea:

           _____

           _____

           _____

           _____

Second main idea: _____

      Details to support second main idea:

           _____

           _____

           _____

           _____

Third main idea: _____

      Details to support third main idea:

           _____

           _____

           _____

           _____

When you finish this paper and have typed your copy, we will mail a copy to this teacher, her principal, and the school superintendent. I promise, you will make this teacher's day!

Figure 7.6
LETTER TO MY FAVORITE TEACHER

Dear Mrs. Smart,

There are many ways that you are my favorite teacher, so listen.

In first grade I remember we had star jars, and you got stars when you read a book. I remember I had eight stars. I think twelve stars could fit in a jar.

I remember when we had centers and recess. That was the best part of the day. In centers I always went to the block center. At recess we would get out our jackets and surf down the slide.

In first grade you taught me how to read. Now I love to read, and I am reading 6th and 7th grade books.

There are several reasons why you are my favorite teacher, and you have only heard a few of my reasons.

Your former student,
Sammy Wills
—3rd grade

the writing process itself—the possibilities are endless. Here are the directions for teaching the class essay:

1. Select a subject from anything that can be classified—classes of foods in nutrition, elements of a short story, reasons to support an opinion, customs of a country in social studies, dialects in a language, books in the library, or different sports. Focusing on the subject, the class should brainstorm and list ideas about the subject on the chalkboard. After exhausting suggestions, adjust, weed out, and

---

Figure 7.7
LETTER TO MY FAVORITE TEACHER

Dear Mrs. Flemister,

Now I am in the third grade, and we are writing a letter to our favorite teacher, and I picked you. There are several reasons why you were my favorite teacher.

First, I liked how you gave us popcorn parties on Friday if we were good. Those were really fun.

Second, I liked how you let me play with the little animals when I was finished early with my work. I could make some good animals out of the modeling clay.

Last, you were always nice and smiling and you never yelled at me. Nobody could make you frown, even when they were bad.

You were my favorite teacher. And I hope you have some good students in your class now.

                                             Love,
                                             Leslie Brown
                                             —3rd grade

---

combine similar topics. The topics that remain become the middle paragraphs of your class essay.

2. Write the main ideas for your middle paragraphs on the chalkboard, and list students' names underneath as they volunteer for a specific paragraph. Let the students get into groups to write their paragraphs. Remind them to craft a good topic sentence and a well-detailed paragraph with real, specific examples. At the end of the period, each group should give their paragraph to the teacher.

Figure 7.8
PREWRITING FOR FAMILY HISTORY STORY

Name: _____

Class Period: _____

Date: _____

Topic: Family History

Prewriting

I. Think of the oldest family member you know that is accessible to you (someone who lives in your town or is close enough for you to talk to.) A grandmother or grandfather or great-aunt or great-uncle would be best. If you don't have an elderly relative still living, think of a friend, a neighbor, or a teacher.

   Record this person's name: _____

II. Take this prewriting sheet home with you. Make arrangements to meet with the person whose name you have written. Record the time and place when you will talk.

Time: _____   Place: _____

III. Ask the person you have chosen all the questions on this sheet, and write the answers on your notebook paper. Bring all these papers back to class with you.

   Questions to ask during your interview:
   1. When and where were you born?
   2. How far back can you trace your family history, and what do you know about your ancestors?
   3. How much did things cost when you were a teenager?
   4. What kind of transportation did people use?
   5. How did you wash your clothes?
   6. Where did you go to school, and how did you get there?
   7. How did you heat your house and school?
   8. What kinds of jobs did people have?
   9. What was your school like?
   10. Do you remember your teachers? What were their names, and what were they like?
   11. How would you compare things today to the way things were then?
   12. Who was your hero when you were young?
   13. What is the most important lesson life has taught you?
   14. Can you tell me one or two stories that would illustrate some of the questions I have asked?

Students may think of and add questions to the interview.

(continued)

Figure 7.8
(continued)

IV. Choose the four most interesting items from your list and draw a circle around them. Or, you may combine several into four sections. This concludes your prewriting.

Rough Draft
For your rough draft, write a family history paper that contains the following paragraphs:

Introduction: Tell a little about the person you interviewed. Include the person's name, place and time of interview, and what they were wearing. Tell a little about yourself and what your relationship is to the person you interviewed.

Next four paragraphs: Write one paragraph each on the four most interesting items you chose from the interview. Be sure to make each paragraph about one-half page long, and include details and direct quotes from the person you interviewed. Be sure to use your quotation marks correctly.

Conclusion: Tell your own feelings about all you have learned from this person.

At that stage, the teacher or students should reproduce each paragraph on a separate sheet of paper, exactly as it was written. Give a copy of each sheet to each student. An option is to use transparencies with an overhead projector.

3. During the next class period lead the class in discussing what order the paragraphs should appear in the final essay. Then, read the paragraphs aloud in the order the class has chosen, exactly as they are.

4. Reading aloud the paragraphs as they are written will show students the importance of transitions. Discuss transitions and how paragraphs have to flow together smoothly and lead logically from one to the next. As a class, rewrite the beginning and ending sentences of each paragraph to create good connecting transitions. You will find as you revise together and create transitions, that other things come up. Working together, you may discover that you have to adjust verb tense, pronoun agreement and reference, parallel structure, and punctuation as you make the form and voice consistent throughout. (Or, each small group could draft transitions and make the paragraphs consistent.)

When I was learning to cook, much of what went on in pots and pans seemed an act of God. Why did cake rise or Jell-o jell or raw eggs thicken into scrambled eggs? I had no idea.

—Judith Moore,
Never Eat Your Heart Out,
p. 244

5. We now have an essay with middle paragraphs but no introduction or conclusion. Stress that the purpose of an introduction is twofold: (1) to keep a writer on the subject, and (2) to get the reader's attention and tell him what to expect. Ideas for writing an introduction are as follows: ask a question and answer it, give a list of facts, tell a little story, or talk in general about the subject. Ask either all students or the groups to write an introduction to the class essay. You might narrow these submitted introductions to the top five or six, read them aloud anonymously, and let the class vote on the one they like best. This way students will *see* which introductions work and which ones don't. Or, you may choose the top two or three introductions and work together as a whole group to combine the best from each to arrive at the introduction the class wants. Again, copy enough of the introductory paragraphs for each student to have one or use the overhead projector.

6. Ask each student or group to write a conclusion for the class essay. The conclusion may be a paragraph that emphasizes the main points in a summary, a paragraph that draws a conclusion, or a paragraph that evaluates. Discourage students from tacking on a moral or a lesson at the end of the essay. Review and finalize the conclusion with the entire class. Type and photocopy the entire essay without making any usage or mechanics corrections.

7. As a class, go over the essay completely and proofread a final time. Check spelling, usage, mechanics, and make any further revisions. Keep working with it until all students in the class are satisfied.

8. Brainstorm titles on the chalkboard and then vote to decide on a title for the essay. Make final copies for everyone and consider submitting it the school literary magazine for publication as a class essay.

Figure 7.9 (p. 155) is a class essay written by an advanced 11th grade class. This essay happens to have five paragraphs, but the form doesn't rely on the number of paragraphs. Figure 7.10 (p. 157) is a 4th grade class essay. The class essay activity is great for teaching a deductive method for planning an essay because it illustrates the steps of

Figure 7.9
PROBLEMS TEENAGERS HAVE TODAY

Being a Teenager in Today's society is a very difficult job. I'm a Teenager, and I know what it's like. It's not all fun and games. There are a lot of hardships, disappointments, and mainly questions that are always weighing us down, usually moral questions of "What's right?" and "What's wrong?" or "What will everyone think of me?" My parents are always saying they know what it is like because they've been there. I don't think so. Teenagers Today have more problems than Teenagers have ever had before.

Parents are a major problem in a Teenager's life. They just don't seem to understand what Teenagers are going Through. They won't let us grow up and make decisions for ourselves. Parents always want to know what's going on and what you're doing. They Think they know what's best for you, and they try to control every aspect of your life. What They have to realize is that Times have changed, and so have we.

Another problem is drugs, often caused by peer pressure. The problem is that once Teenagers Try a drug, they will want to try it again. Once they want it, they can find it anywhere because drugs are easy to get. They can get drugs at school, at work, or anywhere. Drugs Today have a higher addiction level than in the years past. Teenagers are the ones most affected by drugs Today.

Sex also plays a high role in Teenagers' lives Today. When Teens start having sex, there are many problems that could result, such

(continued)

Figure 7.9
(continued)

as pregnancy, AIDS, and other diseases, and even date rape. Statistics say that almost every day at least one teenage girl gets pregnant. This pregnancy leads to instant problems because most teenagers are not financially able to support a child. Every time a teenager or anyone else has sex, he or she has a chance of contracting a disease such as AIDS, which happens to be deadly. Sometimes these sexual acts can lead to date rape. This type of rape can be hard to prove because sometimes the victims are trying to cover up for their actions.

    Teenagers today have more problems than ever before. I think the parents today need to be more understanding and help with these problems. Then teenagers wouldn't ask advice of other teenagers. After all, they don't know anything themselves.

                                         —11th grade

making a list, identifying relationships, formulating a thesis, developing paragraphs with details and transitions, and proofreading.

Class Essay on Our Town

When my students work on a letter-video exchange with students in another state, they like to write a class essay to tell them about Milledgeville. We brainstorm what aspects of our town we should cover and often come up with the following topics: downtown, industry, schools, hospitals, businesses, newspapers, and history. From there, students choose the aspect of the town they want to write about and get into groups to write the paragraph. We continue with the class essay together until we have it ready to mail. Looking at

Figure 7.10
CLASSROOM ANIMALS

We have a lot of different animals in Mrs. Horne's class. These animals make our class fun. Every day we can't wait to see them.

First, There is Patches, our guinea pig. Patches is brown and white and makes a high squeaking sound when we come close to his cage. We take turns taking Patches home for the weekend.

Next is our Tree Frog. We haven't named him yet because we are going to let him go back into nature. He lives in a little glass cage with lots of leaves and branches. We like to feed him crickets.

Last is our parakeet, Kiwi. Kiwi makes a lot of noise in his cage, especially during spelling tests. Mrs. Horne says he is Trying to pronounce the words. He likes to look at himself in the mirror and Turn his head from side to side. Kiwi is a pretty lime green color. That's why we named him Kiwi.

We really enjoy our class pets. We take Turns feeding Them and learning how to take care of them. That's why we like our classroom animals.

—4Th grade

the finished essay, students can see where their group's paragraph fits into the whole. Figure 7.11 (p. 158) lists other subjects for class essays.

Class Essay Using the Senses

Using a place as the subject of an essay, put students into seven different groups. One group should write the introduction, and another will write the conclusion. The five middle groups are

---

Figure 7.11
SUBJECTS FOR CLASS ESSAYS

- Three states of matter (science)
- Three branches of government (history)
- Kinds of music
- Rap artists
- Types of healthy or unhealthy foods

- Types of word problems
- Countries
- Characteristics of countries
- Geography
- Kinds of industry
- Colors (green things, blue things, red things)

- Kinds of rocks
- Kinds of clouds
- Kinds of bones
- Styles of painting

---

assigned one of the five senses, and they write about how they experience the place through their sense (e.g., what they see, hear, smell, taste, or touch). Tell students to include *lots* of sensory detail.

In Defense of Formulas

Formulas, when used as a tool for succeeding in school writing situations, *do* serve a purpose, and it is necessary that we teach them. School writing, then, is important and should be taught, as long as

- ◆ It is not the only kind of writing we teach.
- ◆ It is balanced with freewriting and expressive writing.
- ◆ It is *not* beaten into the ground, year after year in a student's school experience.
- ◆ The purposes for writing various kinds of writing, *including* the five-paragraph theme, are discussed.
- ◆ Variety and creativity are encouraged beyond the skeleton.
- ◆ The method of teaching follows the real writing process, providing for audience (e.g., helping circle used for content, not just for proofreading).
- ◆ A can-do attitude, *not* a can't-do attitude, is conveyed.

Holiday Papers

One way to make school writing more interesting is to connect assignments to events on the calendar. Here are a few ideas.

◆ Mother's Day letter. Figure 7.12 (p. 160) demonstrates a formula letter that 2nd grade teacher Elizabeth Wells assigns her class. Students write a Mother's Day letter to their mothers, but they are told what to put in each paragraph. Their choice comes in the details they choose to put in. A Father's Day letter can be done in the same fashion—a formula with choice.

◆ Turkey letters. Persuasive writing is a requirement in just about every subject. Persuasive letters are great ways to make expository writing more creative. At Thanksgiving, have students pretend to be the turkey and write a letter to the farmer convincing him to let the turkey live; or let the farmer write the turkey a letter explaining why the turkey must die. Figures 7.13 (p. 162) and 7.14 (p. 163) are examples of turkey letters.

◆ Reindeer letter. Another idea is to have a reindeer write Santa a letter asking to be the one to lead the sleigh—instead of Rudolph. Or, a reindeer can write a cover letter and fill out a job application, explaining why she would make a good candidate for Santa's team. When using holidays for writing assignments, remember that not all students celebrate all holidays. Always provide options or alternative assignments.

The cake represents my childhood to me. Mom made the cake for my birthdays, for parties at my elementary school, and for my good report cards.

—Elizabeth Koehler-Pentacoff,

"E. Koehler-Pentacoff," Writers in the Kitchen, *p. 194*

Writing to Learn Across the Curriculum

Students effectively learn content areas through writing. To give them the chance to learn through writing, it's often necessary to deliberately arrange for these occasions. They can learn various subject areas by writing about them—through note taking, using their imaginations, and sharing ideas with one another. I can remember many times in school studying for a test by making study notes—notes I thought I was making to use later for studying. By the time I

Figure 7.12
A MOTHER'S DAY LETTER   *(The writing prompts are in parentheses.)*

Dear Mommy,

(Things That are hard about being a mom) I Think being a mom would be hard. I know you don't like cleaning my room because sometimes it's really messy after I have a birthday party. And you must be Tired of listening To Bayley and me fight. And your back must hurt after scrubbing The floor for Two hours. You must be MAD if you can't put your ears under water when you were on The swim Team. You loved To swim. I know you don't like riding your horse The proper way.

(Things That make my mom laugh) I love To hear my mom laugh when I Tell her a joke and she always starts bursting out laughing. She laughs because it's about Rocky and Bullwinkle on Television. She laughs when I make a funny bunny face and hop around The house like a crazy rabbit. My mom laughs when I dance weird To Christina Agulira, BakStreet Boys, Savage Garden, and Titanic [soundtrack]. She laughs when my horse gets wild and swings around her neck and makes a funny noise. She laughs when I hold my dog and I constantly pour perfume on him. He Tries and Tries To get away. Sometimes he comes home with bows in his hair and painted Toenails. He looked like a girl when he is a boy and my mom started bursting out laughing.

(Things I admire about my mom) I hope I can horseback ride like my mom when I grow up and play The organ for church like my mom does. She plays The organ so smoothly and gets a lot of

(continued)

Figure 7.12

(continued)

compliments. She plays for Two choirs, The children's choir and The adult choir. She gets To play on Two levels. The organ looks very fun, and she gets looked aT a loT when she is playing someTimes. I wanT To play iT so bad. I cannoT sTand iT any longer, and I wish I could play iT.

(The fun parTs abouT being a mom) The mosT fun parT of moTherhood would be waTching me do my reciTals in The NuTcracker and Spring ReciTal. WaTching me play sofTball, when our Team caTches fly balls and when we hiT homeruns and grandslams. She always is proud of our Team. When we win or lose a game she sTill congraTulaTes us. She even congraTulaTes us in pracTice.

(Lessons mom has TaughT me) One special lesson mom has TaughT me is noT calling my broTher names and when he is bugging me To ignore him so we won'T geT in a bigger fighT. She TaughT me To say when he keeps bugging me, "go Take a deep swim" or "go Take a long hike" or "go Take a dump."

(Things I wish for my mom) If I had one wish for my mom iT would be To have The house clean and To have my room clean. To have my broThers room clean. The music room To be clean, dining room, and The furniTure To be clean so you can ride your horse more and noT have To worry abouT guesTs coming To our house.

Happy MoTher's Day!!
Love, your daughTer,
ElizabeTh

—ElizabeTh Craig, 2nd grade

Figure 7.13
TURKEY LETTER

Dear Farmer Tom

    I am a defenseless little Turkey. I have a wife and three eggs. You might as well eat the dog. Please don't eat me. I am much better help alive. Please listen to my plea.

    If you have heard the last health report, you would know beef is better for you. I taste like chicken. Just eat one of them. I taste awful. Turkey makes you very sleepy. Spaghetti O's taste really good. I am nothing but skin and bones. Please don't eat me.

                                                         —6th grade

---

I spent the day following my mother around and observing the way she did everything. When we went to the grocer's, she would point out to me the reason she bought each thing. I was shown a loaf a bread or a pound of butter from at least ten different angles.

—Jamaica Kincaid,
Annie John, *p. 15*

finished making notes, however, there was seldom time left to study. What I didn't realize was that I was learning simply through the act of making the notes. Writing and rewriting helps us to learn and organize new material. The process of writing about a subject helps us to learn it. Any writing in content areas causes this learning to take place, whether it is as simple as recasting the lesson in our own words or as complex as writing a research paper.

Producing an Essay from Memory Research

    Memory research is a useful way to teach the writing of an essay that is *not* a formula; this strategy is more related to the way that practicing writers write nonfiction. Memory research essays can be used across the curriculum and are similar to the childhood memory activity in Chapter 4 (p. 77). Here are the steps for students to perform:

    1. Make a list of three topics they know well enough to write about.

Figure 7.14
No Thanksgiving Feast   *(Note the persuasive devices.)*

Dear Mr. Adams,

You are a very nice man who has a wonderful family and face, and should be Thankful for Them. You and I are a lot alike. We both have wonderful lives and don't want to end Them. Please read This letter with your heart.

If you kill me and have me for your Thanksgiving feast, Think about how my family will feel. They will be sad and lonely, just like your family would be. I would be Thankful if you spared my life.

You know, you don't have to hunt for your dinner. You could much easier go to The Winn Dixie store and buy one. They have already been killed and have already been Through The dreadful moment. Let's not have another death such as These.

This is The Time for giving, not about food. You should be Thankful for what you have and spend Time with your family and friends. You shouldn't spend Time Trying To find The perfect dinner.

By Shelley Watson (Lilly Turkey)
—6th grade

2. Tell a partner about all three topics, mentioning everything they know about the subject.

3. Choose the topic by having the listening partner pick the one with the most detail.

4. Make a list of everything they know about the subject.

5. Organize the list.

6. Write a complete rough draft.

Both the essay from memory research and the class essay are good ideas for using writing to review for specific curriculum on a content-area test. For example, in a history class, the class could write a class essay on the various aspects of the period of history to be covered on the test.

Discipline-Specific Ideas

Writing is a life skill and an exceptional tool for learning; therefore, students need to write in every class. Most of the ideas in this book may be adapted by any teacher in any course, regardless of discipline. The following discussion features some ideas that work particularly well for students as they work in disciplines other than English.

Science

◆ Keep a journal for science class. Since writing helps to reinforce learning and organize it into patterns so that it is learned better, students should write an entry in their science journal every night. In the journal, students should record their understanding of the concepts covered in class. The teacher, if she notices a breakdown in a student's understanding, can review the journal and pinpoint where the understanding has faltered.

◆ Write fantasy or science fiction stories. In creating these stories, students often build on what they know and expand on the possibilities, so this assignment offers insight into students' understanding while giving them a vehicle for exercising their imagination.

◆ Detail personal understanding of concepts in essay form. "Why I Believe in Atoms" and "The Life of a Snail" were the titles of two concept papers that were published in our school's literary magazine.

◆ Write lab reports or abstracts.

◆ Respond with essay answers on tests.

◆ Write reports on books, articles, or television shows.

◆ Create research papers.

◆ Write a play to demonstrate understanding ("Charlie the Corpuscle Traveling Through the Circulatory System").

◆ Craft a commentary or editorial on current events in science.

◆ Practice observation skills by describing a candle burning or a piece of ice melting.

◆ Make a set of directions on how to use various science tools.

In addition, Figure 7.15 (p. 166) lists science writing topics suggested by an elementary teacher. These topics are applicable to all ages.

Physical Education

◆ Read a story about a person not satisfied with his body and have students write how they feel about their own bodies. Consider letting students read other books that deal with body image, such as Paula Danziger's (1998) *The Cat Ate My Gymsuit,* or Judy Blume's (1998) *That Was Then, This Is Now.*

◆ Capture the highlights of a game—whether a gym class playing kickball or the high school team winning the football game. Submit as an essay or as an article for the local newspaper.

◆ Summarize the rules of a favorite sport.

Driver's Education

◆ Capture, in essay form, the action and feelings evoked from seeing a video about an automobile wreck.

◆ Submit reports on the rules of the road—the focus may be on those rules most ignored by drivers or that cause the most injury or accidents.

Foreign Languages

◆ Describe family, house, friends, self.

◆ Write a letter to a pen pal.

◆ Take an imaginary trip and write a postcard home. Extension activities can be writing a travel itinerary and keeping a travel journal.

Figure 7.15
Writing Topics for Science

You are a weather reporter: Give the weather report for today.	The 10-armed octopus
My favorite season	The rattlesnake without a rattle
Clouds	Molly Mae, the mouse
The water cycle	Caught in a thunderstorm
Why zoos are important	Caught in a hurricane
My trip to the moon (or Jupiter or Saturn)	Moose on the loose
Our friend, the sun	Willie, the worm
The strangest sound I've ever heard	Lost in the desert
A day without noise	A day in the life of a seashell, fish, pebble
Sounds in the city or country	I fell off the midocean ridge
My favorite plant	A day on the *Calypso* with Jacques Cousteau
The life cycle of a plant	The fish who lost his way home
If all plants died	The raindrop who never fell
I wonder what a tree sees	Guess what washed ashore?
A day in the life of a brontosaurus or triceratops	Pirate treasure in Lake Sinclair
You are from another planet and have landed on earth	Help! The moon is pulling me!
	An oil spill almost killed me
The day the earth shook	A herring outsmarts the shark
The bashful porcupine	I am no more . . . I am extinct
	You'll never guess what my echo sounder found

◆ Make a list of something; perhaps a wish list, the 10 commandments of dating, or how to survive school.

Math

◆ Keep a journal that details your understanding of mathematic ideas and concepts. Writing about the day's lesson organizes and reinforces learning.

◆ Invent word problems based on real-life situations and show your work as you solve the problems.

◆ Analyze problems and break them down to reach solutions.

◆ Write an essay on how to use math at home or at work.

◆ Explain mathematical definitions—without using the dictionary or textbook definition—to show your understanding.

◆ Write a Friday review of the topics covered during the week.

◆ Write algorithms as a preparation for computer programming and logic development.

Fine Arts

◆ Examine and describe artwork.

◆ Keep a journal of feelings, techniques, and problems encountered and solved.

◆ Compare marching band styles in an essay. Or, compare different forms of bands, such as marching bands and concert bands. Support your choice and record your feelings before, during, and after performances.

◆ Compose lyrics for songs.

◆ Analyze art and music styles.

Social Studies

◆ Summarize a topic in the news.

◆ Write a paragraph to explain a political cartoon.

◆ Write a news report on a significant event in history as if you were a reporter living in that time (e.g., sinking of the *Titanic*, Boston Tea Party).

◆ Read a newspaper and pick out topics that affect us today— list several and develop one fully.

◆ Write a letter to your representative in Congress or the president.

◆ Write an editorial on current events or an article for the school newspaper.

◆ Write a skit for historical role-playing.

◆ Write about your community.

◆ Focus on an event and write about it from two viewpoints.

◆ Write a campaign speech.

◆ Formulate arguments for debate (one or both sides).

The fact of the matter is that I do not really have a recipe for the corn cake I bake. Dona Alda, the wife of Mr. Renato of the Museum, told me how to do it, and in that way I learned, racking my brains until I got it right. (Was it not by loving that I learned to love? Was it not by living that I learned to live?)

—Jorge Amado,
Dona Flor and Her Two Husbands, *p. I*

Figure 7.16
SOCIAL STUDIES WRITING TOPICS

My favorite Georgian (or other state)
Why I'm a proud Georgian (or other state)
Christmas in England
Life on a plantation
You are a mouse on Columbus' ship (or a
    mouse on a slave ship)
The woman or man I most admire
A day in the life of a fireman, postman, or
    astronaut
Dear president, principal, mayor, or senator
Ben Franklin's best invention

My family
A trip to the zoo, farm, country, fire
    department, or airport
Henry Ford's strange invention—the car
You were there with the Wright brothers
I wonder what houses will be like in the
    future
If I were the president
Adventures on an African safari
Astronauts in trouble
Our freedoms

◆ Revise major court decisions or historical events and give reasons for the change.

◆ Pretend to live in a different time and place and write about your experiences.

◆ Pretend to be a famous historical figure and write about your life (perhaps in journal form).

◆ Visit a local cemetery and write about one or more of the people buried there.

Other social studies writing topics suggested by an elementary teacher are featured in Figure 7.16.

English Grammar

Writing about English grammar can extend students' learning. Some students respond and remember grammatical rules if they are used in satire form. A few suggestions for writing about grammar are listed as titles in Figure 7.17 (p. 169).

Summary

School writing is important and must be taught if we are to help students succeed in school. We must, however, teach school writing in

---

Figure 7.17
TOPICS FOR WRITING ABOUT GRAMMAR

Here are a few topics, listed as titles, suggested by an elementary teacher.

- If I Were a Dictionary
- A Day in the Life of a Period
- Why Quotation Marks are Important in Writing
- The Day the Adjectives Skipped School
- My Trip Through the Thesaurus
- No Pronouns Allowed

---

the manner that published writers write. Writing should never be something that students dread or think is a boring thing to do. *All* forms of writing, including school writing, must be interesting, must appeal to the senses, and must come from ourselves and our own locale and memory. When we begin to teach students to write by formulas only and don't allow them to write in a real way, we are denying them part of the richness of life.

Suggestions for the Teacher

◆ Write a timed writing *with* your students, and tell them what you learn by trying this. Figure out together how best to budget time in this situation.

◆ Write a letter to *your* favorite teacher, and mail it! The teacher or a surviving family member would love to read your letter.

◆ Write a "good things about me" paper to share with your students.

Mama's Brownies

2 sticks butter

2 1/2 squares baking chocolate

4 eggs

2 cups sugar

1 cup all-purpose flour, sifted

dash salt

2 teaspoons vanilla

1 cup broken pecan pieces

secret ingredient (2 tablespoons dark Karo syrup)

◆ Preheat oven to 350°. Grease and flour a 9" × 12" aluminum baking pan.

◆ Melt together 2 sticks of butter and 2 1/2 squares of baking chocolate in top of double boiler on top of the stove, or in glass bowl in microwave. Set aside until lukewarm.

◆ In large mixing bowl, beat 4 eggs, and add 2 cups of sugar. Mix well. When butter mixture is cool, add it slowly to eggs and sugar, stirring after each addition. Mix well. Stir in 1 cup of all-purpose flour, sifted, with a dash of salt, 2 teaspoons of vanilla extract, and 1 cup of broken pecan pieces. Mix well.

◆ Just before you pour the batter into the pan, add the secret ingredient: Stir 2 tablespoons of dark Karo syrup into the mixture. Pour the batter slowly, and spread evenly in the pan.

◆ Bake 25–30 minutes. Set pan on wire cooling rack until brownies are cool to touch. Slice with round pizza cutter into large squares. Makes 12–15 brownies.

Identifying the Secret, Essential Ingredients

8

Recipe for Teaching Student Writers

1 part classroom atmosphere

1 part prewriting

1 part helping circle

1 part publishing

1 part making school writing real

1 part fun writing activities

1 part secret, essential ingredients

SPREAD YOUR CLASSROOM ATMOSPHERE UNTIL ALL STUDENTS ARE COVERED. MIX together all parts of the writing process and beat briskly until prewriting, helping circle, and publishing rise to the top. Fold in making school writing real and sprinkle with fun writing activities. Check to be sure all ingredients contain the sense of taste, smell, and texture; the uniqueness of place; childhood memory; and orderly but flexible directions. Add the secret ingredient and stir thoroughly until all parts are blended and real writing is rampant in your classroom.

Each ingredient contains the four qualities successful writers use, and each ingredient works to create the whole. Like some of Mama's recipes, there is, however, another ingredient that makes all the difference. Without this ingredient, your classroom will operate and you can teach writing. With this ingredient, however, students

Then I realized that I, too, have written out my life in recipes.

—Lee Smith,
"Lady Food," We Are What We Ate, p. 203

171

can excel, and they will remember you for years as a teacher who made a difference in their lives.

Recipes

Recipes, just like writing, appeal to the senses; they are specific to our locales, they are intertwined inextricably with our childhood memories and our family stories. In addition, recipes are a list of ingredients and directions that get changed, expanded, or minimized by each cook who uses them. This book contains a recipe for making our students into writers. And later in this chapter you will find the secret, essential ingredient that makes the whole program work—the heart of the matter.

Favorite Teachers

Do you remember your favorite teacher? My favorite was my 4th grade teacher, Mrs. Josey. As a child, I needed a lot of extra personal attention. Every day when we went out for recess, I hid Mrs. Josey's pocketbook from her. Some days I put it in a drawer, others on top of a cabinet, and others under a table. Each day Mrs. Josey came in from break and went on a search for her purse. "*What* have I done with my pocketbook?" she would tease, all along knowing I was the culprit. I am sure that I drove her crazy, but she never let me know it. She showed unconditional love and endless patience. And she gave me the extra attention that she knew I needed.

When I ask teachers to remember their favorite teacher, the answer seldom has anything to do with academics:

- ◆ She taught us how to make quilts in math class.
- ◆ She let us wear her shoes.
- ◆ I was her pet; she told me that she loved me.

If we had a list of the characteristics of teachers' favorite teachers, we would have a wonderful teacher handbook. In fact, we have

Writing, gardening, and cooking are often solitary acts for personal and communal sustenance. . . . Eventually, we savor the layers of pleasure. We need to get the recipes while we can, absorb el pasado, the past, nourishment and delight for the body, for the soul.

—Pat Mora,

"Layers of Pleasure: Capirotada," Through the Kitchen Window, p. 154

much to learn from what we remember about school. We forget so many things, but those things that we remember made an impression on us—either they were taught in a special way or they touched us where it mattered. When students write letters to their favorite teachers, I learn that high school students consider middle school the good old days and middle school students consider elementary school the good old days. I believe this is because as students grow older and move to higher grades, teachers are less nurturing.

Lucy Calkins (1994) writes,

When teachers asked the author Avi, What do we do if our kids won't write?' Avi answered, First you have to love them. If you can convince your children that you love them, then there's nothing you can't teach them.' We fall in love with our students when we know their stories. (p. 17)

Student Writers Have Wonderful Stories

During my years of teaching, I have met many wonderful young writers who do, indeed, have wonderful stories to tell. Here are just a few of their stories.

Steven, Mary, and Thomas

Steven was a student 10th grade with a learning disability that affected his writing. Figure 8.1 (p. 174) is an approximation of how Steven wrote. As you can see, Steven lined up vowels and consonants into various configurations so that, if other students glanced at his paper, his writing would look like theirs.

One day I asked Steven if he thought he could tell a story on the tape recorder. He didn't often talk, but he nodded, took the tape recorder, and went into another room for the class period. After an hour, he brought me the tape recorder and the tape. That night I listened to Steven's tape; Figure 8.2 (p. 175) is exactly what I heard.

"Help yourself!" chirps Marie. "Let's eat all these brownies right up."
"All of them?" he whispers.
"Mmmmmm." She chews fast and noisily. "Don't you just love brownies?"
"I like 'em okay."
"Does your wife make brownies?"
He looks her in the eye. "We have Jell-O."
Marie makes a face. "Nuthin' like a hot brownie."

—Carolyn Chute,
The Beans of Egypt Maine,
p. 79

Figure 8.1
FEELINGS

msl jrTs as asdЄk asdЄlk;
asdk ask asdЄ aek adil
ciae asilЄ casok asok
adijek asdЄk as Єlk
adk adk Єlk asdЄ
werk asdЄkl asЄji ijl l
lk erTTl adsim asdЄim
asdi ewio wer mTT mTTs
admTTs wmTTs

by STeven
—10Th grader
wiTh learning disabiliTy

Steven's story, The Giant Bird, is well-organized with a good beginning, middle, and end. It includes good details, and the writer's voice is evident. Steven's transcribed story is not by a student who can't compose a story. Yet, because of some breakdown between the brain and hand, Steven could not put his stories on paper in the traditional way. After I offered the tape recorder to him as a way of writing, it was as if the dam burst. Steven now had an outlet, so his stories began tumbling out, one after another. One of his stories was published in the literary magazine.

Mary and Thomas were special needs students. Mary had poor motor skills and couldn't move the pencil across the paper very fast. Thomas had great difficulty spelling but had sight knowledge of correctly spelled words. When I gave them computers, Mary was able to type faster than she could write and Thomas made good use of the spelling feature.

Figure 8.2
THE GIANT BIRD

When I was Ten years old, I wenT walking Through some woods with some friends of mine. Melvin, Kenny, Marvin, RoberT, and myself enjoyed playing in The woods.

IT was a windy day, and we were juST walking along, when suddenly a large shadow fell over us. We looked To see who was blocking The sunlighT. Above us was The biggesT bird we had ever seen. (I had never seen a bird ThaT large before, nor have I seen one like IT since.) We ThoughT IT musT be an eagle.

We were so scared ThaT we juST sTarTed running. I ran all The way back To my house and sTarTed To Tell my moTher whaT we had seen. I don'T Think she really believed me.

LaTer eiTher Melvin or Marvin Told me ThaT he had heard ThaT The bird had escaped from a zoo. We Think They caughT The bird, buT we were never really sure. I will always remember The day we saw The gianT bird

—STeven, 10Th grader wiTh learning disabiliTy

Fortunately for Steven, Mary, and Thomas, we have the technology to help them overcome their obstacles to writing. Now we have voice-activated software into which Steven can tell his story and then command the computer to print it. The computer fills in the gap for these students in the same way that a wheelchair fills in the gap for a child who can't walk.

There is a wonderful book for students with special needs written by a man with a learning disability. Christopher Lee's different way of learning was discovered when he went to college. Along with his teacher, Rosemary Jackson, Lee has written a book, *Faking*

It: A Look into the Mind of a Creative Learner (1992). I shared my copy of this book with both Mary and Thomas, and, although these students were not prolific readers, both read it voraciously. After completing the book, they wrote letters to Lee and received responses. It was exciting and enlightening for them to encounter a published author with problems similar to their own.

Sterling

Sterling, an 11th grader, published a story in the *Rain Dance Review* entitled "A Different High School Student." Sterling's story is about what it is like to go through a door in a wheelchair. He describes the way he hopes someone will come to a door at the same time he does, so that they can open it for him. If he is left at the door alone, he tells us in his story, he must use the front pull or the side pull to open the door so that he can enter.

Recently I was walking down the hall beside a student in a motorized wheelchair. Remembering Sterling's story, I hurried to get to the door before the student. Just as I got there, the door swung open. The student had used a remote control to open the door for me. Through reading and sharing stories, like Sterling's story, the world is broadened for students and adults and our tolerance is nurtured.

Scars

When we look at our students, we need to envision Figure 8.3 (p. 177). We need to see that heart inside; even the meanest, hardest students we teach have deep feelings inside. Take note of the qualities exhibited by those teachers we remember decades later and think about which teachers children list as their favorites. Our students may not remember the academics we teach them, but they will always remember how we made them feel. As the Little Prince says, "It is only with the heart that one can see rightly. What is essential is invisible to the eye" (De Saint-Exupery, 1943, p. 70).

"So why does our writing matter again?" [the students] ask.

"Because of the spirit," I say. "Because of the heart."

—Anne Lamott,
Bird by Bird, *p. 237*

Figure 8.3
THE HEART INSIDE

Marvin

But there are just some kids! Marvin was a student who was very difficult to like, much less to love. He would let his pants down in class to tuck his shirt in. He would burp out loud. He would talk about gang activity and pretend to shoot the other students with a gun. He would talk back to me, one of my pet peeves. Needless to say, I was having a difficult time with Marvin.

Then I learned that Marvin's grandmother was dying of cancer, so I began to ask him about her. When she died, I called the house and talked with Marvin.

When Marvin returned to school, his freewrite was a beautiful tribute to his grandmother. I took that freewrite home, typed it in calligraphy font, and printed it out on pretty paper. Then I took it to the library and had it laminated, and I put it on Marvin's desk.

When Marvin came to school the next day, he found it there. He never said anything to me about it, and I never said anything to him. But from that moment, Marvin changed. He felt himself loved and he began to *act* loveable. By the end of that year, Marvin and I did love one another.

Adding the Secret, Essential Ingredient

Many years ago I had a very special dream. In my teacher dream, I am at the bottom of a huge mountain. All around the mountainsides are little caves, and in each cave is a child, asking to get out. I go from cave to cave, slowly working my way to the top of the mountain. But the opening to each of the caves is too small; I can't get in, and the children can't get out. Finally, I reach the top of the mountain and find a young boy. I sit down beside him, and he points to the countryside below, moving his arm in a sweep as if telling me something important. It is as if he is saying, "See? It's all very easy, when you do it this way." It was the child who was teaching me. The dream showed me that teachers must learn from students.

One of the many things I have learned from my students is that they are constantly changing. Teachers can never think that we have it all figured out. We need to be flexible enough to do for and with each new group what *that* particular group needs. Students will always be our teachers, too.

What is the secret ingredient to teaching writing? We cannot teach children anything well if we do not love them. Teachers are salespeople, and we are often trying to sell something our students do not want to buy. We need to greet *all* our students (even the most difficult to *like*) with love. As Og Mandino (1977) says in his book, *The Greatest Salesman in the World*:

> And how will I confront each whom I meet? In silence, and to myself I will address him and say I love you. And who is there who will say nay to my goods when his heart feels my love? (p. 61)

We smiled and shyly touched each other's elbows with fingertips and said to each other about our canning what we said to each other about our children, "How pretty, how pretty."

—Judith Moore,
Never Eat Your Heart Out,
p. 118

Our job as teachers is to help our students find their spot in this world, and writing can help them do that. We must share ourselves with them, for we are their models. We must share our memories, our families, and, yes, our recipes . . . to show them how to write, to show them how to love. As the Velveteen Rabbit learns from the Skin Horse in the nursery, "Real isn't how you are made . . . It's a thing that happens to you. When a child loves you for a long, long time—not just to play with, but *really* loves you, then you become real" (Williams, 1991, p. 17). When you are real, when you have loved your students and you know your students' stories through their writing, even the most difficult students become beautiful.

Suggestions for the Teacher

◆ Tell your students about your favorite childhood meal, and ask them to tell you about theirs. Post recipes around the room.

◆ Learn something from your students every day.

◆ Tell (and show) your students you love them, and watch what happens.

References
and Resources

Agee. J. (1938). *A death in the family*. New York: Vintage Books.

Amado, J. (1969). *Dona Flor and her two husbands*. New York: Alfred A. Knopf.

Atwell, N. (1989). *In the middle*. Portsmouth, NH: Heinemann.

Avakian, A. V. (Ed.), (1997). *Through the kitchen window: Women writers explore the intimate meanings of food and cooking*. Boston: Beacon Press.

Ayres, M. (1997). "The parable of the lamb," In A. V. Avakian (Ed.), *Through the kitchen window: Women writers explore the intimate meanings of food and cooking* (pp. 155–161). Boston: Beacon Press.

Blume, J. (1998). *That was then, this is now*. New York: Puffin Books.

Brande, D. (1934). *Becoming a writer*. New York: Harcourt Brace.

Calkins, L. M. (1994). *The art of teaching writing*. Portsmouth, NH: Heinemann.

Capote, T. (1996). *A Christmas memory, one Christmas, and the Thanksgiving visitor*. New York: Modern Library.

Chute, C. (1985). *The Beans of Egypt, Maine*. New York: Ticknor & Fields.

Coss, C. (1997). My mother/her kitchen, In A. V. Avakian (Ed.), *Through the kitchen window: Women writers explore the intimate meanings of food and cooking* (pp. 13–16). Boston: Beacon Press.

Danziger, P. (1998). *The cat ate my gymsuit*. New York: Putnam.

De Saint-Exupery, A. (1943). *The little prince*. New York: Harcourt Brace.

Elbow, P. (1978). *Writing without teachers*. New York: Oxford University Press.

Esquivel, L. (1992). *Like water for chocolate*. New York: Doubleday.

Finerman, W., Newirth, C., Starkey, S., Tisch, S. (Producers) & Zemeckis, R. (Director). (1994). *Forrest Gump*. [Film]. Hollywood, CA: Paramount Pictures.

Fisher, MFK. (1908). *The art of eating: The gastronomical me*. New York: Simon & Schuster, Macmillan.

Flagg, F. (1987). *Fried green tomatoes at the whistle stop café*. New York: McGraw-Hill.

Frank, M. (1995, rev. ed.). *If you're trying to teach kids how to write, you've gotta have this book!* Nashville, TN: Incentive Publications.

Freeman, M. (1998). Martha Freeman. In T. Gardella (Ed.). *Writers in the kitchen: Children's book authors share memories of their favorite recipes* (p. 4). Honesdale, PA: Boyds Mills Press.

Gardella, T. (1998) *Writers in the kitchen: Children's book authors share memories of their favorite recipes*. Honesdale, PA: Boyds Mills Press.

Gibbons, F. (1998). F. Gibbons. In T. Gardella (Ed.). *Writers in the kitchen: Children's book authors share memories of their favorite recipes*. Honesdale, PA: Boyds Mills Press.

Goldberg, N. (1991a). *Writing down the bones*. New York: Bantam Books, 1991.

Goldberg, N. (1991b). *Wild mind: living the writer's life*. New York: Quality Paperback Book Club.

Gordon, C., & Tate, A. (Eds.). (1960). *The house of fiction* (2nd ed.). New York: Charles Scribner's Sons.

Gordon, N. (1984). *Classroom experiences: The writing process in action.* Portsmouth, NH: Heinemann.

Hall, N. (1994). Interactive writing: Its nature, purpose and scope. In N. Hall and A. Robinson (Eds.), *Keeping in touch: Using interactive writing with young children* (pp. 1–30). Portsmouth, NH: Heinemann.

Haynes, D. (1998). Chinese spareribs. In M. Winegardner (Ed.). *We are what we ate: 24 memories of food* (pp. 110–122). New York: Harcourt Brace & Company.

Harris, J. B. (1998). In a leaf of collard, green. In M. Winegardner (Ed.). *We are what we ate: 24 memories of food* (p. 105–109). New York: Harcourt Brace & Co.

Huddle, D. (2000). *Writers ask.* Portland, OR: Glimmer Train Press.

Hughes, L. (1940). Salvation. In *The Big Sea: An Autobiography* (pp. 18–21). New York: Hill and Wang.

Hughes, L. (1996). Thank you, ma'am. In A. S. Harper (Ed.), *Langston Hughes short stories* (pp. 223–226). New York: Hill and Wang.

Hurston, Z. N. (1978). *Their eyes were watching God.* Chicago: University of Illinois Press.

Jansen, S. (1997). Family liked 1956: My mother's recipes. In A. V. Avakian (Ed.), *Through the kitchen window: Women writers explore the intimate meanings of food and cooking* (pp. 55–64). Boston: Beacon Press.

Jensen, E. (1996). *Brain-based learning.* Del Mar, CA: Turning Point.

Kavasch, E. B. (1997). My grandmother's hands, In A.V. Avakian (Ed.), *Through the kitchen window: Women writers explore the intimate meanings of food and cooking* (pp. 104–108). Boston: Beacon Press.

Kincaid, J. (1985). *Annie John.* New York: Farrar Straus Giroux.

Kirby, D., & Liner, T., with Vinz, R. (1981). *Inside out: Developmental strategies for teaching writing.* Portsmouth, NH: Boynton/Cook Publishers.

Koehler-Pentacoff, E. (1998). E. Koehler-Pentacoff. In T. Gardella (Ed.). *Writers in the kitchen: Children's book authors share memories of their favorite recipes* (pp. 194–195). Honesdale, PA: Boyds Mills Press.

Krim, N., & Worsham, S. (1993, April). Team-teaching long distance: Making connections across the Mason-Dixon line. *English Journal,* 16–23.

LaMeres, C. (1990). *The winner's circle: Yes, I can!* Newport Beach, CA: LaMeres Lifestyles Unlimited.

Lamott, A. (1995). *Bird by bird: Some instructions on writing and life.* New York: Doubleday.

Landon, L. (1999). *Dinner at Miss Lady's: Memories and recipes from a southern childhood.* Chapel Hill, NC: Algonquin Books.

Lee, C., & Jackson, R. (1992). *Faking it: A look into the mind of a creative learner.* Portsmouth, NH: Boynton/Cook, Heinemann.

Lee, H. (1960). *To kill a mockingbird.* New York: J. B. Lippicott.

Lowry, B. (1998). Entrée nous. In M. Winegardner (Ed.), *We are what we ate: 24 memories of food* (pp. 126–134). New York: Harcourt Brace.

MacLeish, A. (1977). In G. Plimpton (Ed.), *Writers at Work: The Paris Review Interviews,* second series (p. 130). New York: Penguin Books.

Macrorie, K. (1976). *Telling writing* (2nd ed.). Rochelle Park, NJ: Hayden.

Mansfield, K. (1956). Prelude. *Stories* (pp. 52–98). New York, Alfred A. Knopf.

Mandino, O. (1977). *The greatest salesman in the world.* New York: Bantam Books.

Mason, B. A. (1998). "The burden of the feast." In M. Winegardner (Ed.), *We are what we ate: 24 memories of food* (p. 134–145). New York: Harcourt Brace.

Mehta, G. (1998). The famine of Bengal. In M. Winegardner (Ed.). *We are what we ate: 24 memories of food* (pp. 156–157). New York: Harcourt Brace.

Minnich, E. K. (1997). But really, there are no recipes. In A. V. Avakian (Ed.), *Through the kitchen window: Women writers explore the intimate meanings of food and cooking* (pp. 134–147). Boston: Beacon Press.

Moffett, J., & McElheny, K. R. (Eds.).(1966). Afterward. In *Points of view: An anthology of short stories* (pp. 566–574). New York: New American Library.

Moore, J. (1997). *Never eat your heart out*. New York: Farrar Straus Giroux.

Mora, P. (1997). Layers of pleasure: Capirotada. In A. V. Avakian (Ed.), *Through the kitchen window: Women writers explore the intimate meanings of food and cooking* (pp. 148–154). Boston: Beacon Press.

Murray, D. (1968). *A writer teaches writing*. Boston, MA: Houghton Mifflin.

Perrine, L. (1970). *Story and structure*. New York: Harcourt, Brace & World.

Plimpton, G. (Ed.). (1977). *Writers at work: The Paris review interviews* (2nd series). New York: Penguin Books.

Plimpton, G. (1989). *Writers chapbook: A compendium of fact, opinion, wit, and advice from the 20th century's preeminent writers*. New York: Viking.

Prenshaw, P. (1984). *Conversations with Eudora Welty*. Jackson, MI: University of Mississippi Press.

Proust, M. (1934). *Remembrance of things past*. New York: Random House.

Rain Dance Review. (1982–2001). Milledgeville, GA: Baldwin High School.

Rugg, H. (1963). *Imagination*. New York: Harper & Row.

Sanders, D. (1995). *Dori Sanders' country cooking*. Chapel Hill, NC: Algonquin.

Shelnutt, E. (1989). *The writing process: Keys to the craft of fiction and poetry*. Atlanta, GA: Longstreet Press.

Smith, L. (1998). Lady food. In M. Winegardner (Ed.), *We are what we ate: 24 memories of food* (pp. 201–204). New York: Harcourt Brace.

Smyth, M. (1997). Hedge nutrition, hunger, and Irish identity. In A. V. Avakian (Ed.), *Through the kitchen window: Women writers explore the intimate meanings of food and cooking* (pp. 89–94). Boston: Beacon Press.

Spark, M. (2000, December 25). My Madeleine. *The New Yorker*, 105–110.

Stein, S. (1999). *How to grow a novel*. New York: St. Martin's Press.

Ueland, B. (1987). *If you want to write: A book about art, independence, and spirit* (2nd ed.). St. Paul, MN: Graywolf Press.

Viorst, J. (1987). *Alexander and the terrible, horrible, no good, very bad day*. New York: Simon & Schuster.

Walker, M. (1989). Memory. *This is my century: New and collected poems* (p. 49). Athens, GA: The University of Georgia Press.

Williams, M. (1991). *The velveteen rabbit*. New York: Doubleday.

Williams, S. (1993, October). Making winners of the no-win track. *English Journal 82*, 6, 51–56.

Williams, W. C. (1951). *The collected earlier poems of William Carlos Williams*. New York: New Directions.

Williams, W. C. (1951). The red wheelbarrow. *The collected earlier poems of William Carlos Williams*. New York: New Directions.

Winegardner, M. (Ed.). (1998). *We are what we ate: 24 memories of food*. New York: Harcourt Brace.

Worsham, S. (1996, May–June). Five good writing ideas. *Teachers and Writers*, 9–12.

Acknowledgments

In addition to my mother, to whom this book is dedicated, I want to
thank my daddy, whose constant creativity is with me today and
whose hard work and dedication made so many opportunities
available; my sister Linda and my brother-in-law Tom, for being my
champions and always cheering me on; and my large and loving
extended family for filling my life with stories. I also acknowledge
my teachers, especially Mary Josey in 4th grade, for giving me the
attention I craved; Sarah Gordon, for teaching me to write "the real
way" and Ken Kantor, for teaching me to *teach* that way. I thank
my students for teaching me that love is the whole point; David
Greenberg, for teaching me how to share my message with others;
Anne Meek for bringing my book out of its hiding place; my friends
at ASCD for much tender loving care in getting my book into teachers' hands; and my friend Elizabeth Horne, whose belief in me
never wavers and who inspires me with her motto: If you can dream
it, you can do it.

Index

Page numbers followed by an *f* indicate reference to a figure.

About the Author

A CLASSROOM TEACHER OF 30 YEARS, WITH BOTH GIFTED AND AT-RISK STUDENTS, Sandra Worsham presents workshops to writing teachers all over the country. She was Georgia's 1982 Teacher of the Year, a 1992 Milken National Educator, and is a member of the National Teachers Hall of Fame. In addition to her work with students grade 9 through 12, Worsham has conducted more than 100 workshops with elementary and middle school students and their teachers.

A fiction writer, Worsham has published several short stories and articles and has won a grant to write a novel. In 1999, she edited a collection of community stories gathered by her students, published in *Everybody Has a Story to Tell: Stories from Flannery O'Connor's Milledgeville.* Worsham originated the *Rain Dance Review* at the high school about 20 years ago and a countywide writing program, the *Celebration of Writing.*

Contact Sandra Worsham at 1908 Robin Circle, Milledgeville, Georgia 31061. She can be reached by phone at (478) 452-4031, or by e-mail at sworsham@alltel.net.